By the end of the decade, every midsize town and major city in America will have a multiple-location or multiple-venue church. Everything you need to know about getting started in multi-site strategy is in locations. This is the book to read!
—Jim Tomberlin, former multi-site pastor of Willow Creek Community Church, South Barrington, Ill.

This book is a great read for any church that has a heart to see the kingdom grow through its influence in its own community and beyond.
—Henry Schorr, Centre Street Church, Calgary, Alta.

This book contains a wealth of information and resources for churches considering multi-site ministry.
—Adam Hamilton, United Methodist Church of the Resurrection, Leawood, Kans.

The multi-site church is not just another passing fad but a revolutionary remaking of the church. This book is a must-read.
—Robert Lewis, Fellowship Bible Church, Little Rock, Ark.

We are thrilled to be part of a multi-site church revolution. Our video worship venues were such a success that we launched more, and on Easter 2006 we launched our first off-campus worship site.
—Gerald Sharon, Saddleback Church, Lake Forest, Calif.

We are honored that this groundbreaking book tells our story, showing how we are part of a larger movement of multi-site churches across the country.
—David J. McDaniel, North Point Community Church, Alpharetta, Ga.

When we decided to become a multi-site church, it was our friends at Leadership Network and the research which resulted in this book that helped us to reinvent our church to reach even more people for Jesus.
—Mark Driscoll, Mars Hill Church, Seattle, Wash.

When George Whitefield told John Wesley that he needed to take the church to the people, a worldwide revival resulted. That same impulse is behind the multi-site movement, and this book brings out the heart for taking the church to where the people are already gathering.
—Dottie Escobedo-Frank, Cross Roads United Methodist Church, Phoenix, Ariz.

This is one of those books that comes along once in a generation. It will reshape the churchscape by giving tens of thousands of churches the map they need to become multi-site.
—Mark Batterson, theaterchurch.com, Washington, D.C.

If I could give every church leader only one book this next year, this would be it!
— Dave Ferguson, Community Christian Church, Naperville, Ill.

If you want to understand the rationale, benefits, and challenges of multi-site, and to see some practical examples of how it works and where it's heading, this book is for you.
— Larry Osborne, North Coast Church, Vista, Calif.

When we made the move to become a multi-site church, we did so without the benefit of a book like this. I'm sure it will inspire you to grow a healthier church wherever you are.
— Dino Rizzo, Healing Place Church, Baton Rouge, La.

The Leadership Network Innovation Series

Confessions of a Reformission Rev.: Hard Lessons from an Emerging Missional Church, Mark Driscoll

The Multi-Site Church Revolution: Being One Church in Many Locations, Geoff Surratt, Greg Ligon, and Warren Bird

Other titles forthcoming

the multi-site church *revolution*

BEING ONE CHURCH . . .

. . . IN MANY LOCATIONS

geoff surratt

greg ligon

warren bird

ZONDERVAN®

GRAND RAPIDS, MICHIGAN 49530 USA

ZONDERVAN.COM/
AUTHOR**TRACKER**

The Multi-Site Church Revolution
Copyright © 2006 by Geoff Surratt, Greg Ligon, and Warren Bird

Requests for information should be addressed to:

Zondervan, *Grand Rapids, Michigan 49530*

Library of Congress Cataloging-in-Publication Data

Surratt, Geoff, 1962 –
    The multi-site church revolution : being one church in many locations / Geoff Surratt, Greg Ligon, and Warren Bird.
        p. cm. — (The leadership network innovation series)
        Includes bibliographical references and index.
        ISBN-13: 978-0-310-27015-7
        ISBN-10: 0-310-27015-4
        1. Church facilities—Planning. 2. Church management. I. Ligon, Greg, 1962 – II. Bird, Warren. III. Title. IV. Series.
    BV604.S87 2006
    254—dc22

                                                2005034544
    CIP

Interior design by Nancy Wilson

Printed in the United States of America

06 07 08 09 10 11 12 • 10 9 8 7 6 5 4 3

Contents

114280

Part Three:
What Makes Multi-Site Work Best

Part Four:
Why Extend Further and Reach More People?

Foreword

My journey into the multi-site approach began back in 1988. My work was primarily focused on the urban poor, and I was dealing with the complex issues of welfare incomes and urban crisis. Our first site was the result of a building project that I am told was the first urban redevelopment initiated by a church since "white flight" began in the community surrounding our church. Our second location was the result of negotiating with a rapidly declining congregation. They owned a poorly maintained facility built sometime around the 1950s.

We became a two-campus congregation, one English-speaking and one Spanish-speaking. One was predominately African American, the other was first-generation Latinos. We realized the tremendous potential in penetrating the urban corridor, if we could somehow partner with established churches that were quickly declining and that would sometimes leave behind even massive facilities.

I wish I could tell you the story ended well, but as often happens, our first experiment is more failure than success. In the end, the pastors preferred overseeing their own campuses. After I left, they became independent churches.

We found that even certain and impending extinction was not motivation enough for most congregations to seriously consider allowing their facilities to be used for a new community of faith. What we learned was invaluable.

I have become convinced that we can do a lot more together than we can apart. The power and synergy of an interconnected network of churches held together through vision and values is far more greater than the segmentation and disconnectedness of our present system.

The multi-site movement is a strategic response to the question of how to maintain momentum and growth while not being limited to the monolithic structure of a megachurch. Think about it this way: What would happen if the gift of leadership were available not to just one location but to an entire city? I think we should be honest enough to admit that leadership gifting as demonstrated by individuals such as Paul Yonggi Cho, Rick Warren, Kirbyjon Caldwell, and Bill Hybels is rare and unique.

The multi-site strategy allows that level of leadership gifting to elevate the effectiveness not only of one campus but of an endless number of potential kingdom localities. The possibilities are limitless, especially with contemporary technology.

Today, nearly twenty years after my first multi-site experiments, I find myself in what I consider the most exciting and strategic city in the world: Los Angeles. To accomplish all we have in mind, it's not simply beneficial but essential for us to engage the city from multiple locations.

Multi-site is not simply about space; it's about place. Our multi-site strategy is more of a cultural acupuncture. It's not about how big you are; it's more about being a finely tuned instrument positioned exactly where it can have the greatest impact.

We presently have four locations: one north, one east, one west, and one downtown. From our nightclub downtown (club Mayan) to our gathering at Beverly Hills High School, each location affects a part of the cultural dynamic of LA that the other campuses could not.

The challenge, of course, is leadership. No matter what your strategy, leadership is always the primary issue.

We know of many others who are having amazing success through video venues and we sit back in amazement. We've chosen an on-site-teaching approach, maybe because we're in the capital of film, television, and video. My personal dream is to raise up the next generation of great communicators. Certainly Los Angeles needs it; I think even the whole world needs it too.

Whatever approach you choose, this is a conversation that must be had. For too long the local church has diffused its effectiveness by operating in isolation especially, in major world-class cities. It's time to consider an approach that can harness energy, resources, vision, and talent, and create a synergistic approach committed to expanding the kingdom of God, bringing the world into relationship with Jesus Christ, and turning the cities and the future upside down.

—Erwin Raphael McManus
Cultural Architect, Mosaic (www.mosaic.org)
Founder, Awaken (www.awakenhumanity.org)

Preface

A Prediction for the Future

Among Protestant churches in the United States:
- Well over 1,500 churches are already multi-site.[1]
- One out of four megachurches is holding services at multiple locations.[2]
- One out of three churches says it is thinking about developing a new service in a new location.[3]
- Seven out of the country's ten fastest-growing churches offer worship in multiple locations, as do nine of the ten largest churches.[4]

The multi-site movement is represented in every area of the country, across many denominations, and in churches of all sizes, especially those with attendances of 250 and up. The dramatic growth of interest in the multi-site approach is nothing short of a revolution in how to reach people for Christ.

After a frustrating family vacation involving too many nights at motels that were unclean and unfriendly, a businessman in Tennessee came up with a novel idea. He would create a trusted network of family-friendly hotels across the country, all with the same name. "What should we call it?" he asked his art director. "Holiday Inn," came the reply, since the man had recently seen the 1942 movie *Holiday Inn*, starring Bing Crosby and Fred Astaire.[5]

The idea was an immediate winner. The public knew the film and had good associations with the name. People liked the idea of a hotel chain where you could always count on experiencing the same quality level and finding a core of common features, such as an on-premises restaurant and a child-friendly environment.

The idea of a hotel network was right for the times, and soon other hotel entrepreneurs began their own chains. In the 1950s, when the first series of Holiday Inns were built, 98 percent of hotels were stand-alone, single-entity hotels with names like "Grove Tree Inn" and "Lakeside Hotel," according to Kemmons Wilson, the son of Holiday Inn's founder. Today it's the opposite. Some 80 percent of hotels are part of recognized brands like Holiday Inn, Marriott, Hilton, and Omni, with the other 20 percent remaining as one-location independent or boutique hotels, Wilson says.

The same thing happened with restaurants (McDonald's, Burger King, and Shoney's Big Boy all began in the 1950s) and more recently with banking, office supply stores, and many other types of business. How many of us visited the new Olive Garden restaurant in our own town because we had previously visited or heard something good about another Olive Garden?

Overview of the Future

The prediction of this book is that multi-site extensions of trusted-name churches are something that connect well with today's times. Many such extensions are already being birthed across the United States. Some are citywide—such as Mosaic in Los Angeles, with four different campuses at Mosaic Mayan (in downtown LA), Mosaic Pasadena, Mosaic Beverly Hills, and Mosaic Chino—some are regional, and some national. Chances are that one or more multi-site churches will soon form in *your* city, and perhaps your own church will join or create one of these multiple-location clusters.

The primary motive behind the multi-site approach is to obey the church's God-given directives. The Great Commandment (Matt. 22:37–39) is to love God and one another, the Great Commission (Matt. 28:18–20) is to make disciples of all nations, and the Great Charge (1 Peter 5:1–4) reminds us to involve all believers in ministry. Drawing from Scripture and over fifty different contemporary examples, *The Multi-Site Church Revolution* shows you how any church, regardless of its size or location or denomination, can contribute to fulfilling these essential commands by developing an identity as one church in many locations—not just one crazy church in your area but many "crazy" churches across your town. Fifty years ago, the one-venue option was the norm. Fifty years from now, we believe multi-venue and multi-site will be the norm.

Part 1 of this book describes the beginnings of the multi-site movement. You'll meet some of the early pioneers and see what a highly successful multi-site church looks like. You'll look in vain for a one-style-fits-all mentality; instead, you'll see that a wide variety of models have emerged.

Part 2 explains how a church becomes one church with two or more locations. What motivates a church to do so? What are the typical trigger points? How is the vision cast? How are the new sites funded?

Part 3 assesses the factors that make a multi-site church work well. You'll learn how a church can ensure a successful DNA transfer (vision and core values) to its new site, how new leaders are developed, and how structure and staffing change. You'll examine the ways many multi-site churches use technology to support elements of their worship services. You'll also identify the primary reasons churches succeed, as well as how they overcome common snags.

Part 4 asks what happens when a church adds a third, fourth, or fifth site. What changes when a church meets in ten or twenty different locations? Here you'll grasp the heart of those whose dream is to develop an entire movement of replicating campuses. You'll dream with those who seek to turn the tide in a battle that the current approach to church seems to be losing. Then you'll be challenged to consider the specific steps you'll take with your church.

Appendix A points you to some very practical resources that are available online. Appendix B reminds us that other countries are way ahead of churches in North America in developing multi-site ministry. And appendix C provides a directory of the multi-site churches cited in this book.

The Revolution Has Begun

We predict that 30,000 American churches will be multi-site within the next few years, which means one or more multi-site churches will probably be in your area. The press is taking note of the growing multi-site movement, from Christian magazines like *Christianity Today*[6] and *Leadership Journal*[7] to dozens of major newspapers, including the *Chicago Tribune*[8] and the *Dallas Morning News*,[9] as well as television shows like *Religion and Ethics Newsweekly*[10] and radio programs like National Public Radio's *All Things Considered*.[11]

Churches are learning new ways to multiply and extend their ministry without having to pour millions of dollars into new buildings. They are moving into their gyms and multi-purpose rooms and then across town into theaters, schools, and empty warehouses. They are becoming "one church, many congregations," reaching hundreds and even thousands of unchurched people they might never have reached had they not branched out.

We estimate that one-third of the churches in America could succeed as multi-site congregations. The most likely candidates will emerge from churches with these qualities (some churches may match two or even three of these categories).

- Up to 20 percent (one out of every five) need to consider multi-site immediately because they are growing and face lack-of-space problems, whether seating or parking or both. Multi-site might save these churches huge amounts of money that would otherwise be poured into a facility-expansion program.
- Up to 20 percent (one in five) could successfully experiment with multi-site using a low-risk approach. Lyle Schaller, dean of American church consultants, advises, "Half of the congregations in North America need to expand their weekend worship services."[12] A portion of those expansions could be in new locations rather than expanding the facilities where regular Sunday morning services are held.
- At least 5 percent (one in twenty) regularly use image magnification to foster a more intimate congregational connection with speakers and singers, and could therefore easily make the transition to a multi-site videocast format, whether live or recorded. "We estimate that some 25,000 congregations are currently using image magnification," says Ron English, founder and president of Fowler Productions (www.fowlerinc.com). "We are a visual society and we are rapidly becoming screen oriented. I am a firm believer that the more personal you can create worship and preaching for the individual believer, the more impacting will be the result."

With one out of three churches seriously looking into multi-site, a revolution is afoot in how the church reaches new people for Christ. This book is the story of that revolution. In an extremely practical style, this book will guide a church in answering the question, "How could God use *our church* if we were open to joining this 'revolution'?"

Turn the page to find out what churches like yours are already doing.

Part

One

the **birth** *of the* multi-site movement

You Say You Want a Revolution?

Meet several highly successful multi-site churches

> These men who have turned the world upside down have
> come here also.
> — Acts 17:6 ESV

It is coming ... a movement of God. Some even call it a revolution.

On Sunday morning at Seacoast Church, where I (Geoff) serve on staff in Charleston, South Carolina, a band launches into a hard-driving worship chorus as lyrics and background images are projected on screens and television monitors throughout the auditorium. Everyone begins to sing along with the worship team.

This describes the experience at many contemporary churches, except that this scene happens eighteen times each weekend in nine locations around the state, all of which are known as Seacoast Church. Using many different bands and worship leaders, Seacoast's eighteen nearly identical weekend services represent the look of a church that chose not to fight city hall in order to construct a bigger building. We instead continued to reach new people by developing additional campuses.

At another church across the country, a congregation just north of San Diego sings "How Great Thou Art" in Traditions, one of six venues on the same church campus. North Coast Church in Vista, California, developed six different worship atmospheres, all within a few feet of each other. Traditions is more intimate and nostalgic, while other venues range from country gospel to a coffeehouse feel to vibrating, big subwoofer attitude.

The elements unifying these six on-site venues are the message (one venue features in-person preaching, and the others use videocasts) and the weekly adult small groups, whose discussion questions center on the sermon that everyone heard, no matter which venue they attended. North Coast has now developed multiple venues on additional campuses, so that on a typical weekend in early 2006, worshipers chose between more than twenty different services spread across five campuses.

Over in Texas, Ed Young Jr., senior pastor of Fellowship Church in Grapevine, preaches every Sunday morning on four campuses — Grapevine, Uptown Dallas, Plano, and Alliance — all at the same time. Ed delivers his Saturday night message in person in the main sanctuary on the Grapevine campus. It is videotaped and viewed the following morning by congregations at the other venues via LCD projectors and giant projection screens, framed by live music and a campus pastor. "We decided we could reach more people and save a huge amount of money by going to where the people are and doing smaller venues instead of building a larger worship center in Grapevine," Ed says.

In downtown Chicago at New Life Bridgeport, a small church meets in a century-old former United Church of Christ facility. The pastor, Luke Dudenhoffer, preaches a sermon that he's worked on with up to ten other pastors across the city. Each pastor leads a satellite congregation of New Life Community Church, which is known as one church in many locations.

At Community Christian Church in Chicagoland, eight different drama teams perform the same sketch at eight different locations. Then up to three different teachers deliver a message they've developed collaboratively. Most services have an in-person preacher, though some sermons are videocasts.

These churches, and more than 1,500 churches like them across the country, are discovering a new model for doing church. Going beyond additional service times and larger buildings, churches are expanding into multiple venues and locations, and many of them are seeing increased evangelism and even exponential growth as a result. The approach of taking one church to multiple sites seems to be the beginning of a revolution in how church is done in North America and around the world.

> The approach of taking one church to multiple sites seems to be the beginning of a revolution in how church is done in North America and around the world.

When four university computers were linked together for the first time on something called ARPANET in the fall of 1969, there was very little press coverage of the event. Aside from the scientists working on the project, no one considered this event revolutionary; it was just an adaptation of concepts that had existed for many years. In spite of such simple beginnings, ARPANET, known today as the Internet, has revolutionized almost every aspect of our lives in the twenty-first century—from how people get sports scores to how they buy airline tickets to how they size up a church before visiting it.

Revolutions often begin with little fanfare. They are usually built on concepts that have existed for many years and are seldom recognized in the beginning as revolutionary. The measure of a revolution is its impact, not its origins.

That is why we believe the multi-site church movement is revolutionary. The concept of having church in more than one location isn't new or revolutionary; the roots of multi-site go back to the church of Acts, which had to scatter due to persecution. Elmer Towns points out that the original Jerusalem church "was one large group (celebration), and many smaller groups (cells).... The norm for the New Testament church included both small cell groups and larger celebration groups."[1] Likewise, Aubrey Malphurs observes that Corinth and other first-century churches were multi-site, as a number of multi-site house churches were considered to be part of one citywide church.[2]

> The measure of a revolution is its impact, not its origins.

Multi-Site Overview

What is a multi-site church? A multi-site church is one church meeting in multiple locations — different rooms on the same campus, different locations in the same region, or in some instances, different cities, states, or nations. A multi-site church shares a common vision, budget, leadership, and board.

What does a multi-site church look like? A multi-site church can resemble any of a wide variety of models. For some churches, having multiple sites involves only a worship service at each location; for others, each location has a full range of support ministries. Some churches use video-cast sermons (recorded or live); others have in-person teaching on-site. Some churches maintain a similar worship atmosphere and style at all their campuses, and others allow or invite variation.

What kind of church uses the multi-site approach? The multi-site approach works best for already growing churches but is used by all types of churches. The majority of multi-site churches are suburban, but many can be found in urban contexts and some in rural contexts. Multi-sites are found among old churches and new, mainline and nondenominational, and in all regions of the country. Smaller churches (30 – 200 people) tend to do multi-site as a niche outreach or as a regional-campus approach. Medium-size churches (200 – 800 people) that go multi-site tend to have only two or three campuses. Larger churches (800 – 2,000 people) and megachurches (2,000 people and up) are the most likely to be multi-site and to do it in a way that develops a large network of campuses.

Why become multi-site? The purpose of becoming a multi-site church is to make more and better disciples by bringing the church closer to where people are. The motivation is to do a better job of loving people, including different types of people, with an outcome of making significant advances in obeying Jesus' Great Commandment (Matt. 22:37 – 40) and Great Commission (Matt. 28:19 – 20).

How long do multi-site churches last? Several churches have been multi-site for up to twenty years, and a handful for even longer. Some churches use a multi-site approach as a transitional strategy during a building program or a seasonal outreach. Other churches intentionally choose to be multi-site only temporarily as a church-planting strategy to help new congregations start out strong.

Until recent years, few churches in this century have purposely pursued a multi-site strategy. In fact, many churches in the movement have stumbled into multi-site almost by accident. The potential impact of the multi-site movement, however, is extraordinary. Even though the movement is still in the very early stages, multi-site churches are beginning to have a significant influence on how people are being reached with the good news of Jesus Christ.

For Most Churches, Multi-Site Is a "God Thing"

True to historic movements, this new paradigm is finding expression around the world, across all denominations, church sizes, and structures. Churches with 20, 200, 2,000, and 20,000 attendees are experimenting with the "one church in many locations" idea, while denominations are testing multi-site as both a church revitalization model and an alternative to customary church-planting models.

The multi-site movement, however, isn't confined to the suburbs or to the opening of new locations for growing churches. Urban churches facing the prospect of closure due to dwindling membership are being revitalized as they become satellite campuses of a growing congregation elsewhere in their city. Rural churches are expanding into other communities in their region as they continue to grow in their own town or village. The impact of multi-site churches of every size, shape, and denominational background is just beginning.

It seems to be happening everywhere, with each church having a different trigger point.

After preaching the two Saturday evening services, Craig Groeschel went home with his pregnant wife, Amy, and in the middle of the night, they headed to the hospital for Amy to give birth to their fourth child. Craig was not going to make it for the next morning's services in their fast-growing congregation, Life Church in Oklahoma City (which stylizes its name as LifeChurch.tv).

Now what? they wondered back at the church. Someone had a crazy idea: "Hey, let's roll the video from Saturday night." That decision proved to be divinely inspired.

"'Life Church even extended itself to Phoenix in July 2005. How can a church in one location "jump the fire trail" almost one thousand miles like that? It starts with the church's leadership being convinced that it is something God wants them to do as part of their mission.

A multi-site approach is well suited to fast-growing congregations like Life Church, and high-visibility congregations tend to be the ones highlighted in the recent wave of media attention to the multi-site movement. But far more churches are flying under the media radar. They come in all sizes and settings, but their results are equally as impressive.

Take, for example, twenty-five-year-old Chartwell Baptist Church in Oakwood, Ontario, a suburb of Toronto, where Peter Roebbelen is pastor.

"We backed into multi-site," says Peter. "It's not something we intentionally tried to do. It was more like a disruptive moment when we faced a problem and saw an opportunity." In essence, their problem became an opportunity.

For Chartwell, the initial motivation for becoming multi-site was to accommodate growth. "We needed to go to a third service, but we wanted to do it during the optimal Sunday morning time," Peter explains. So Chartwell began experimenting with the use of additional campuses. That was in 1993. Ten years later, Chartwell was offering six Saturday night or Sunday morning services on four campuses. By 2005, more than 1,200 people regularly attended one of the Chartwell congregations, yet the original church's seating capacity was 260 — and still is — which is consistent with their particular strategy of creating a sense of relational intimacy within each local worship setting.

> "We backed into multi-site. It was more like a disruptive moment when we faced a problem and saw an opportunity."
> — Peter Roebbelen

Life Church and Chartwell are typical of how a congregation becomes multi-site. Most churches that use a multi-site approach evolve into it, rather than starting out with it.

According to our research at Leadership Network, the 1,500-plus multi-site churches across North America become multi-site by extending themselves to more than one location: some to locations across town, some across the state, and some around the world.

Church analysts have been observing this trend for a number of years, which was initially seen only in the more innovative churches.

In the 1990 book *Ten of Today's Most Innovative Churches* by Elmer Towns, three of the ten featured churches have modeled, during some part of their recent history, the practice that the book calls "one church meeting in many locations … a multi-staffed church, meeting in multi-locations, offering multi-ministries, with a single identity, single organization, single purpose, [and] single force of leadership."[3]

Most churches that use a multi-site approach evolve into it, rather than starting out with it.

Peter Roebbelen is one of the few people who has researched the development in recent years. Using a study grant from the Louisville Institute[4] (funded by the Lilly Endowment), he visited a number of different locations. His analysis? "I think this is a true movement, a true new work because it's popping up in independent situations all over the place at about the same time, literally around the world."

The people he interviewed don't seem to be fad driven. "It's a God thing," Peter concludes. "Most didn't sit down to strategize and plan and then conclude, 'We're going to try multi-site,' because none of us had heard of multi-site. We simply began doing it. The stories have been remarkably similar from coast to coast and from north to south."

Especially Helpful for Fast-Growing Churches

Among the ten fastest-growing churches in the United States, 70 percent use multiple venues or multiple campuses. Likewise, among the ten largest churches in the United States, 90 percent use multiple venues or multiple campuses (see the tables on pp. 22–23). Among megachurches in general, 27 percent hold services at off-site locations, according to a 2005 research project on megachurches.[5]

Some megachurches continue to build and fill huge sanctuaries. Willow Creek, Chicago, moved into a new 7,100-seat auditorium in 2004; Salem Baptist, Chicago, built a 10,000-seat mega-facility in 2005; Lakewood Church, Houston, bought and refurbished the 16,000-seat Compaq Center sports arena in 2005; First Baptist Church, Woodstock, Georgia, finished a 7,000-seat sanctuary in 2005; Without Walls, Tampa, bought a 9,000-seat Lakeland campus *and* a 3,000-seat Auburndale satellite campus in 2005; and Glory Church of Jesus Christ, a Korean-American congregation in Los Angeles, bought and

America's Ten Fastest-Growing Churches (Fastest-growing church listed first)		
Multi-Site?	**Church Name**	**City/State**
Yes	Without Walls International Church	Tampa, FL
Yes	Mount Zion Baptist Church	White Creek, TN
No	Lakewood Church	Houston, TX
Yes	LifeChurch.tv	Oklahoma City, OK
Yes	Saddleback Church	Lake Forest, CA
Yes	The Fountain of Praise	Houston, TX
Yes	Second Baptist Church	Houston, TX
Yes	Franklin Avenue Baptist Church	New Orleans, LA
No	Prestonwood Baptist Church	Plano, TX
No	Fellowship of the Woodlands	The Woodlands, TX

Adapted from *Outreach*'s 2005 annual ranking

moved into a 7,000-seat former boxing arena, known as the Grand Olympic Auditorium, in 2006. (Two of these congregations — Willow Creek and Without Walls — have at least one other campus as well.)

The bigger trend, however, is toward smaller auditoriums. As sociologist Scott Thumma told National Public Radio's *All Things Considered*, "Many of the very large megachurches are beginning to spin off satellite or branch campuses around the city or area as a way to reach their diverse populations but also so they don't have to continue to invest in larger and larger buildings."[6]

Not a Growth Strategy by Itself

Bill Easum and Dave Travis have observed that the genius of multi-site is not that it grows your church but that it keeps your church growing. In their book *Beyond the Box: Innovative Churches That Work*, they comment, "The key to understanding the multi-site movement is to remember that fulfilling the Great Commission drives these congregations, not a growth strategy."[7]

In short, multi-site is a means toward an end, not an end goal in itself. Most churches do generate growth through multi-site, but just

America's Ten Largest Churches (Largest church listed first)		
Multi-Site?	*Church Name*	*City/State*
No	Lakewood Church	Houston, TX
Yes	Without Walls International Church	Tampa, FL
Yes	Saddleback Church	Lake Forest, CA
Yes	Second Baptist Church	Houston, TX
Yes	New Birth Missionary Baptist Church	Lithonia, GA
Yes	Willow Creek Community Church	South Barrington, IL
Yes	World Changers Church International	College Park, GA
Yes	Southeast Christian Church	Louisville, KY
Yes	Potter's House	Dallas, TX
Yes	Fellowship Church	Dallas, TX
	Adapted from *Outreach's* 2005 annual ranking	

as importantly, multi-site keeps them from capping the growth they're experiencing.

Multi-Site Churches Are Bridging Today's Gap

In recent decades, American churches have morphed from seeker-driven to purpose-driven to postmodern models, all as a response to the skyrocketing number of unchurched Americans and the constant need to apply a biblical worldview to current contexts. Church attendance did increase slightly (from 42 percent to 43 percent), but the actual number of unchurched adults has nearly doubled in the last fifteen years, currently numbered at 75 million.[8] The net result is that despite the sincere prayers and efforts of thousands of pastors and leaders across the country, current models of church growth are not working well enough. We must continually find new ways to bridge that gap.

The new multi-site approach, from all early indications, is beginning to do just that. "Early indicators show that multi-site churches are more evangelistic than those with one site," reports Thom Rainer, a prominent consultant and church researcher.[9] A survey we helped

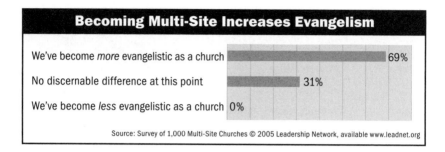

Becoming Multi-Site Increases Evangelism

We've become *more* evangelistic as a church	69%
No discernable difference at this point	31%
We've become *less* evangelistic as a church	0%

Source: Survey of 1,000 Multi-Site Churches © 2005 Leadership Network, available www.leadnet.org

conduct in 2005 (see the table above) found that churches have a greater evangelistic impact when they become multi-site.

The many reports of conversion growth at multi-site locations affirm that something is working well. Many people who are wary of "established religion" are willing to come back to these same churches in one of their multi-site expressions, as seen in this email Seacoast Church recently received:

> I am twenty-five years old and have spent the majority of my life questioning religion and Christianity. My wife, however, has always been an amazing Christian woman and example to me. She attended a service [at Seacoast] last year, and she was so touched that she insisted I go. I told her I would go with her, [although] I was as far from a relationship with Jesus Christ as a person could be. I left that service at the West Ashley Campus moved by [Pastor] Greg's words, relatability [sic], and sincerity. I felt like, and have since that first service, that each message was delivered solely for me. I do not know how to thank you all for bringing Christ into the life and spirit of a twenty-five-year-old atheist.

Churches are discovering the power of multiplication as they begin to grow beyond the four walls of the box they built. Moving beyond the traditional outreach and discipleship model of multiple services and larger buildings, they are embracing the concept of "one church with many congregations." And the revolution is just beginning. Imagine the impact of thousands of people in your town committing their lives to Christ for the first time. Imagine churches in your community whose attendance either has plateaued or is in decline finding new life as they partner with growing churches to reach the lost. Imagine the impact as the revolution crosses cultural and international boundaries to reach people who have never been exposed to the good news of the gospel.

The reasons for choosing to become a multi-site church are as varied as the multi-site expressions that have evolved, but the vast majority of multi-site congregations are finding the experience to be a solid win for their mission as a church. The next several chapters will illustrate how the multi-site approach is being used in a wide variety of settings across North America, the lessons learned, the pitfalls to avoid, and how *your* church can join the revolution.

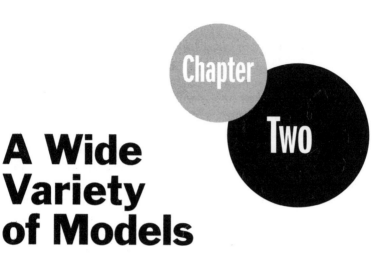

A Wide Variety of Models

Notice the broad range of models in this overview of the multi-site movement

I have become all things to all people so that by all possible means I might save some. — 1 CORINTHIANS 9:22

Several years ago, I (Geoff) attended my first church-growth conference at a megachurch in the Midwest. I heard for the first time about using drama in weekend services, utilizing secular tunes to connect with seekers, and preaching topical sermon series drawn from everyday life. I was convinced this was exactly what my fifty-member rural Texas church needed. I went back to the buckle of the Bible Belt and threw away all the hymnals, opened the Sunday service with a pantomime of a man spinning plates, and kicked off my Life in the Fast Lane sermon series with a screaming cover of the Eagles tune of the same name. The chosen few (soon to be fewer) were not amused, nor spiritually edified. I quickly discovered that what worked really well a thousand miles away in Big City, Illinois, didn't necessarily play in

Small Town, Texas. When it came to reaching out to lost people, one size certainly didn't fit all.

The same is true of multi-site churches. The model that works great in Seattle's exurbia may not fly in downtown Miami. The model that fits inner-city Philadelphia may not draw the same response in center-city Vancouver.

But the underlying principle of the multi-site strategy is easy to understand and relatively simple to adapt. It's simply a way to build on tools we've already put into service to Christ. The logic works like this: most North Americans are familiar with the idea of doing multiple services in the main sanctuary (or equivalent), such as Sunday morning at 9:30 and 11:00, and perhaps Saturday evening as well. But what happens when a church expands further to include:

- An on-premises additional venue, such as a video venue in a multi-purpose room
- An off-premises satellite or branch or regional-campus location, such as a school or a converted warehouse across town
- A partner church, whether in the same community or halfway around the world, with the staff, style, or content coming from the initial campus and the partner church identifying itself as a site of the initial campus

The term *multi-site* covers all these concepts, up to the point of starting a totally new church. A church's new site might sponsor all the same ministries as the initial campus, or it might offer only worship services. The common thread is that the church "happens" at more than one location.

In short, *multi-site* summarizes today's approach to church in which geography is no longer the defining factor. Gone is the day when gatherings must happen on Sunday mornings and in a church sanctuary (or equivalent) with a steeple on top for it to be called "church." Both Christians and the general public have accepted this reality. Theologians have always known it, often reminding us that the word *church* in the Bible refers not to a building with a pulpit, classrooms, and a fellowship

Definition of Multi-Site Terms

Multi-site church: Short for multiple-site church, or one church with multiple locations. A church is considered multi-site if it has more than one worship venue, more than one campus, or a combination of both.

Campus: Any location where a complete church ministry (i.e., adult worship, nursery, children's programming) takes place. A multi-site church may have several campuses.

Branch or satellite: An off-site campus.

Venue: A location where a worship service for adults is held, such as a church's fellowship hall, gym, or chapel. For example, Saddleback Church has one campus in Lake Forest, CA, but that campus currently has seven venues for adult worship.

Worship service: Christ-centered community that usually includes singing, praying, and preaching. It happens regularly, usually weekly. Also known as a celebration, service of divine worship, worship experience, and sometimes simply "church."

Strategic partner: At North Point Community Church in Atlanta, where this idea is most actively being pioneered, a strategic partner is a church that shares North Point's mission, strategy, values, and beliefs but remains a separate entity.

Note: In this book, a "multi-site church" is one that develops *worship* communities in multiple locations. Many churches sponsor off-site ministries (for example, helping out weekly at a local soup kitchen), but those alone do not create one church in many locations. Likewise, when we cite weekly worship-attendance numbers in this book, we mean the number of adults and children who participate in a worship service during a typical week, without counting anyone twice.

hall but to people called to be part of a community also known as the body of Christ.

Churches Are Tailoring Multi-Site to Their Own Mission

The variety of ways in which churches today can adapt the multi-site approach is unlimited. In an interview with Charles Arn, author of *How to Start a New Service*[1] and president of Church Growth, Inc. (www.churchgrowth.net), he told us, "I can't help but imagine where the multi-site idea may take us in twenty years. The possibility of churches communicating their message in multiple locations has the potential of extending the gospel in dramatic new fashion. The process is simply an application of Paul's own life and model, 'I have become all things to all people so that by all possible ways I might save some'" (1 Cor. 9:22).

The core idea for the multi-site movement is rather simple: one church in multiple locations. Yet the outward expression is often more like a smorgasbord than a single-niche restaurant chain. This is not a McDonald's franchise movement in which all menus look alike. While each campus shares an intentional sense of "brand identity" and resembles the original campus in some profound way, few multi-site churches come across as an exact duplicate of the initial church.

Five Models

One of the things that helped me (Geoff) early on in the multi-site journey at Seacoast was being a member of Leadership Network's first group in the Multi-Site Churches Leadership Community. (I liked it so much that I'm currently leading the fourth group.) What was invaluable to our team was the ability to look at other models. We peeked under the hood, kicked the tires, and quizzed the designers of other models. In the end, we were able to walk away with some great ideas that have now been incorporated into the way we do it at Seacoast. No church had the ideal approach for us, but each had something we could learn from. As Tom McGehee, founder of the WildWorks Group (www.wildworksgroup.com), says, "No model is perfect; but some are useful."

When asked, "Is there an approach or model that works best?" we have been hard pressed to identify such. There are many models, seemingly almost as many as there are conversations about multi-site churches. Each week we hear from churches that are new to the multi-site movement, and with each conversation comes a new angle or facet of being multi-site. That being said, for the purpose of providing some "handles" for exploring the models presented in this book, we have identified five broad categories as follows:

Five Models for Multi-Site Churches	
Video-Venue Model	Creating one or more on-campus environments that use video-cast sermons (live or recorded), often varying the worship style
Regional-Campus Model	Replicating the experience of the original campus at additional campuses in order to make church more accessible to other geographic communities
Teaching-Team Model	Leveraging a strong teaching team across multiple locations at the original campus or an off-site campus
Partnership Model	Partnering with a local business or nonprofit organization to use its facility beyond a mere "renter" arrangement
Low-Risk Model	Experimenting with new locations that have a low level of risk because of the simplicity of programming and low financial investment involved but that have the potential for high returns in terms of evangelism and growth

Video-Venue Model

One popular model is to develop video venues where the sermon is presented via videocast, which is prerecorded more often than live. A video-venue model allows churches to extend their reach by creating a variety of environments, often driven by worship style, that attract different segments of their communities. This approach has been well received by churches large and small.

At North Coast Church in Vista, California—one of the country's pioneers of this model—the weekend's teaching pastor always preaches in the venue called North Coast Live. In the rest of the locations and venues, worshipers watch the message on video. At North Coast, a video venue is a site with a targeted worship experience that is unique to that venue. It is not an overflow video-fed room but a positive experience with live worship, in some cases food and coffee, and an in-person host. During the teaching time, a full-screen videocast of the teaching pastor's message is shown. Each of the venues has the feel of a small to medium-size church yet shares the resources of a large church.

> Each of the venues has the feel of a small to medium-size church yet shares the resources of a large church.

"Church leaders often assume that their people would never settle for a sermon delivered by video," says Larry Osborne, lead pastor at North Coast, which has been doing video-venue worship services since 1998. "In reality, that initial resistance is usually offered by people who've not experienced a video venue firsthand," he says. He notes that early marketing surveys showed no interest for minivans, microwave ovens, or fax machines because it's hard for people to imagine the usefulness of something they've yet to see.

It turns out that worshipers at North Coast love the video-venue approach. On a typical weekend, two-thirds of them choose to worship at a venue where the sermon is presented via videocast rather than at North Coast Live, which has in-person preaching. More than twenty services are held each weekend, and only three of the services have the preacher in the room; for all other services, the preacher's message is presented via videocast.

One reason people respond so well to videocast sermons is that North Coast makes the experience the opposite of being a punishment or a second-class overflow-room environment. Churches have for many years used extra spaces as places to handle overflow crowds. They are often unattractive, out-of-the-way, and ill-fitted locations. The unintentional message being conveyed is, "If you are late, you get a cheap seat in a room where no one would choose to sit." The result is competition for the perceived primo seats and lots of disgruntled people. The video-venue model addresses all these negatives by creating a desirable location that has its own intrinsic values associated with worship style, group size, and other environmental factors.

Our experience at Seacoast is much the same. Cumulatively, we three authors have experienced worship via videocast in over fifty churches and venues, done with varying levels of technological expertise. To date, we have yet to experience a time when people did not laugh, cry, or otherwise respond the same way to the digital image they were viewing as they might have responded if they were present at the original in-person setting. One of our favorite stories is that of David McDaniel, executive director of campus expansion at North Point. David says that Andy Stanley preaches in person at their Buckhead campus four or five times a year. When he does, David will consistently have as many as fifty people tell him after the worship service, "It was nice to see Andy, but bring back the video!" The larger-than-life videocast of Andy's teaching enables them to see and hear more clearly, leading to a more powerful spiritual experience.

In other churches, the preacher changes locations, and so does the video. For example, at Bethlehem Baptist Church in Minneapolis, Minnesota, preaching pastor John Piper rotates between their two campuses on Sunday morning, and the "opposite" campus plays a videocast of his message, which is recorded at the Saturday evening service where he preaches every week.

In recent days, as technological advances have occurred, some churches connect two or more campuses to create live simulcast experiences, which some call two-way worship or "concomitant" worship. For example, at Northland–A Church Distributed, in the Orlando area, its four campuses share simultaneous worship. Two campuses are connected by broadband lines that enable them to have part of their worship team on each campus. Another campus twenty-five miles away uses wireless microwaves to connect to the other campuses. Their unique use of technology in the video venues makes a strong contribution to living into the reality of being one church in multiple locations.

Regional-Campus Model

Do you find that while members of your church may be willing to commute a long distance to come to church, they seem unable to bring their unchurched friend that same distance? Likewise, do you find that the farther away your members live from your worship site, the less likely they are to come to midweek activities on your church campus? These questions are central to the regional-campus model, in which a church extends its reach by replicating the experience of the original campus at additional campuses so that the experience is accessible to people who do not want to or cannot make the long commute to the original campus. This approach is used in many settings, both small and large.

Portland

New Life Church, a Conservative Baptist congregation in the West Linn suburb of Portland, Oregon, has had an average weekly attendance of 200–300 people for the last fifty years. "We live in an anti-growth community," says Scott Reavely, senior pastor. "They're not going to let us expand."

But the church, which is very supportive of overseas missions, is keenly aware of the spiritual needs of its community. So it took a very bold step: in 2005 it opened a second campus four miles away, with very positive results. "Doing this has forced us to be more evangelistic," Scott says, "and non-Christians seem to like the idea of us starting small neighborhood congregations rather than trying to grow bigger in one location."

"We're trying to be incarnational," explains Nathan Pylate, the campus pastor of New Life's new site. "We want to maximize the ways we can touch people, and the additional-campus approach gives us more 'coastline.' It helps us better meet the needs of people in our neighborhood."

The multi-site approach in West Linn—New Life Church Riverfalls, New Life Church Robinwood, and perhaps other New Life branches to come—provides far more flexibility than being an independent church plant would. "Emotionally, there was significant resistance to saying goodbye to people we've known for many years, and financially, it would be devastating to send out a large portion of our givers," Scott says. "Now I feel free to encourage my best givers and best workers to go to our new sites without the fear that we as the sending location will never recover."

The spiritual fruit has been wonderful. In its first few months as a multi-site body, the church saw an unprecedented level of prayer at the original campus and more people were baptized than in any previous year during the last two decades.

Chicago

At the heart of Willow Creek Community Church's values is evangelism—turning irreligious people into fully devoted followers of Christ. This happens as friends bring nonbelieving friends to a worship experience designed to meet them where they are and then move them toward Christ. For some twenty-plus years, it has worked very well.

When Willow's leadership conducted a survey as it prepared for a huge capital campaign to enlarge the base needed for their next twenty years, they asked questions to the effect of, "Are people far from God getting saved at our church? And if the lost aren't getting found, what are we doing wrong?"

After studying the findings, Bill Hybels, the founding pastor, made an important discovery: "People who live beyond the thirty-minute mark rarely invited nonchurched people as their guests and had a much lower frequency rate for midweek participation. They had a lower volunteerism rate and a lower small group involvement. Their children weren't as involved either." The conclusion? "We were incapable of fulfilling our mission as a church for those who lived farther away from the South Barrington campus." This discovery became the primary incentive behind their decision to develop regional campuses. They realized that something had to be done differently if they were going to continue to fully live out their evangelism value.

> "We were incapable of fulfilling our mission as a church for those who lived farther away from the South Barrington campus."
> — Bill Hybels

Bill knew that for this idea to work, it would need strong leadership. That's when he invited Jim Tomberlin to join the team. Jim came armed with leadership skills honed by starting and leading a large, growing congregation in Colorado Springs. Jim was charged with the assignment of "figuring out what this thing would look like" and then "making it happen"—both tall orders.

Jim began with the vision of creating a way to provide the "Willow experience" within a thirty-minute drive time of anyone in greater Chicagoland. Out of this vision was born a regional strategy centered on the development of campuses that mirror what happens at the original campus in South Barrington. The first steps were taken toward execution as they identified the Chicago suburb of Wheaton for the first regional campus.

Once this decision was made, the real work began. Jim recounts the challenges of convincing the Willow staff that people do exist who have leadership gifts and would be willing to lead a campus but not preach! How could this be? Other bumps in the road occurred as Jim approached members of the South Barrington team asking about the possibility of recruiting members of their teams (small groups, children's ministry, men's ministry, women's ministry, etc.) to serve in staff positions at the new campus. Commitment to vision met practical reality when faced with the cost of losing seasoned team members. In the end, Jim assumed the temporary role of campus pastor at Wheaton, and in doing so, he literally created the model that would be replicated as Willow extended to four campuses to date, with a fifth likely to launch in downtown Chicago shortly after the release date of this book.

Most churches that are employing the regional-campus model provide not just a worship service but a full-service campus. When a campus is launched at Willow Creek, you experience all that you would on the South Barrington campus, down to the Seeds bookstore in the lobby of their leased facilities, where attendees can purchase tapes of services.

Indianapolis

Yet another example of the regional-campus model is Eastern Star Church in Indianapolis, where Jeffrey A. Johnson Sr. has been the senior pastor since 1988. Their approach, as outlined by deacon and chief operating officer Robert Wright, is to be one church in three locations circling the city of Indianapolis. On those Sundays when the senior pastor preaches in all three locations, beginning his first sermon around 9:00 and ending his final one around 2:00, he blazes across fifty miles of back streets and interstate highways and delivers close to three hours of preaching to eight thousand people. Four very strong choirs rotate locations on a preset schedule. They lead the praise and worship each Sunday, and the same order of worship is followed at all three locations. The congregation is tied together by a very tight administrative and organizational structure and by consistent written communications to its members.

Both satellite locations were selected based on membership demographics derived from a zip-code survey—which points, as at Willow, to the importance of a shortened drive time. This approach at Eastern Star allows more members to serve and more opportunities for leaders to be developed at each location. The outreach of the church is extended to new neighborhoods and growing areas of the community. At each location, the worship ministries and other leadership can grow in areas such as ushers, tape ministry, nurse's ministry, pastor's aid, Sunday church school and Children's Church, bookstore ministry, café ministry, parking ministry, and sacred dance ministry.

Teaching-Team Model

As soon as a church begins to explore the idea of multiple venues or campuses, "Who will the teaching pastor be?" is one of the first issues that must be addressed. Community Christian Church, where Dave Ferguson is lead pastor, is one church with eight sites locally and seven sites nationally. In becoming multi-site, they needed to figure out how to handle the teaching.

From early on in the process, Dave didn't want the expansion of the church to be limited by the number of places where he could physically be. His solution was to develop a teaching team who would work through the following issues together:

- What are we going to teach next week? Next month? Next year?
- What do we want all the families in our church to understand and experience?
- How can we get the whole church focused on one topic or theme each week?
- What can we do to make sure that what happens during the weekend makes a difference during the week?
- Is there a way to get everybody on the same page? Adults? Kids? Students? Music? Media? Theater?

The transition to multi-site led them to create an innovative teaching-team model they call The Big Idea. Community Christian is now one network of churches (www.newthing.org) extending from Denver to New York City, with teaching teams, creative artists, and curriculum writers collaborating to deliver high-impact celebration services and small groups for children, students, and adults that all focus on one weekly theme called The Big Idea. While sharing the week's Big Idea, the worship team and teaching team will slightly customize their styles to meet the needs of their target community.

The teaching-team model allows churches to extend their reach by leveraging a strong teaching team across multiple venues and sites, whether the teaching is live or recorded. Many multi-site churches feature on-site preaching delivered by a team of teaching pastors. Most of those have one regular preacher for each site. Other churches have their preachers rotate between sites: Pastor Smith preaches one week at Trinity West, the next week at Trinity East, and the next week at Trinity South. When the preachers rotate, a second person — a campus pastor — is usually based at the extension site so that the people have the same "face with the place" each week.

As a church adds more locations, the same pattern continues but usually not so simply. For example, First Baptist Church of Windermere, a multi-campus congregation just south of Orlando, launched its third campus in September 2004. Mark Matheson provides overall leadership for the church. He is also the campus pastor for Windermere Community Church. Chuck Carter is campus pastor at Windermere Baptist Church, a second campus. Rick Pughe is campus pastor at another campus known as Lake Buena Vista Baptist Church. Each campus pastor also serves as the primary preaching pastor for his campus and preaches there in person most weeks. (A more extensive profile of this church is given in chapter 4.)

Partnership Model

One of the most significant innovations in the multi-site movement is the development of powerful collaborative partnerships. Numbers of churches are extending their reach by deciding to partner with an existing organization to use its facility. The list of options is long, including prisons, fire stations, planned neighborhoods, local restaurants, community centers, hospitals, and more. One example involves collaboration with a religious organization whose roots were highly evangelistic: the Young Men's Christian Association, known today as the YMCA.

Stillwater United Methodist Church in Dayton, Ohio, is a church with many blessings. A growing, involved membership is just one of those blessings. When an opportunity to grow even more presented itself, the church took a leap of faith and never looked back. It started several years ago when lead pastor Duane Anders answered a phone call from the vice president of the area YMCA. When the caller mentioned he was seeking donations to fund a new space for a local YMCA, Duane commented that his church would like to use the new space too. The vice president took Duane seriously and said the YMCA organization would be open to the idea of partnering with the church so resources could be shared.

Stillwater worked out an agreement: a pastor's office would be located in the Kleptz YMCA; the church could place a sign on the property and could meet on Sunday mornings and use the building one weekend evening a month. This expansion was christened Livingwater United Methodist Church. Although Livingwater has its own pastor, Stillwater considers itself one church with two locations.

John Alice is the campus pastor at Livingwater. John says having his office in the hub of the Y gives him great opportunities to share his ministry. People are always walking by, sticking their heads in to say hello, or stopping in to chat. New YMCA members on orientation tours are introduced to John as well. When people hear he is the Y's pastor, they often stop by to find out more about the church. This campus has a chance to reach out to those who would not normally be in a typical church setting but would be willing to check out their spiritual curiosity in a more neutral site, such as the YMCA. The nontraditional setting of the YMCA may make John more approachable for people who are struggling with their faith, or lack of it.

> "'We don't want to be renters, but partners in your ministry.' And they are wide open to us as we help the YMCA fulfill the spiritual aspect of their mission statement."
>
> — Duane Anders

The initial partnership, primarily defined by shared use of the YMCA facilities, continues to evolve. As the YMCA began to expand their program, a decision was made to establish a morning and afternoon preschool program. The YMCA's challenge was lack of space! The solution was to use the classrooms at Stillwater that were largely unused on weekdays. The decision was made, the lease payment from the church to the YMCA went away, and the partnership deepened. In recent days, the YMCA and the church have created a shared staff position and hired a leader to serve students.

This amazing collaboration boils down to a good relationship, according to Duane. "We told the Y, 'We don't want to be renters, but partners in your ministry.' And they are wide open to us as we help the YMCA fulfill the spiritual aspect of their mission statement."

Low-Risk Model

The low-risk model allows churches to extend their reach through rapid expansion. They accomplish this by development of sites and venues that have low risks because of the simplicity of the programming and low financial investment involved. The low-risk model also carries the potential for high returns in terms of growth. This model is embodied by Dave Browning and the team at Christ the King Community Church (CTK) in the Skagit Valley region, between Bellingham and Seattle, in Washington.

"In 1999, I was encouraged by the leadership at CTK in Bellingham, Washington, to launch CTK of Skagit Valley thirty miles south," Dave says. In the Skagit Valley, some 150,000 people are distributed among numerous small townships. CTK determined that if their goal was to effectively reach out to thousands of unchurched people in the valley, they would have to do that in more than one place. "It didn't take long to realize that more communities than just Mount Vernon (the largest in the valley, with 20,000 people) could benefit from a CTK-type ministry, and we began establishing worship centers here, there, and everywhere," Dave says. "McDonald's has sold billions of hamburgers. How many could they have sold if they had remained in one location?"

Dave launched the church in 1999, with 134 people at its first service, going to two services that fall and three in January 2000. By the end of CTK's first year, thirty-eight small groups were convening weekly in Jesus' name for Bible discussion, prayer, friendship, support, and encouragement and outreach. CTK launched new worship centers in 2000 (two), 2001 (one), 2002 (one), 2003 (five), 2004 (three), and 2005 (four).

By the end of 2005, Christ the King was sponsoring locally 26 services on 17 campuses, each in a different town, totaling 3000 weekly worshipers. Three different languages are used, and the services in English are not identical. "By decentralizing the church and using smaller venues, we are able to have different services at different times with different teachers in different locations," Dave summarizes.

Christ the King's low-risk philosophy basically says, "If one leader is passionate about having the Christ-the-King experience in their community, we will start a site." The CTK team surfaces these leaders in a number of ways. Many leaders come to them, desiring to connect to the work that CTK is accomplishing. In other cases, CTK has placed simple ads in local newspapers, asking if readers were interested in being a part of a new kind of church. The ads stated: "Are you an entrepreneurial Christian leader? Ready for a new kind of church in your area? Willing to be a strategic partner to make it happen? If your mission, vision, and values intersect with ours, then we're praying that you'll meet with us."

The CTK team then meets with anyone who shows up at the designated meeting place (usually a public facility that they can use at no cost) and—voilà!—the core group is established. A leader is identified, and through coaching, the team develops and then multiplies this initial group. When the number of groups reaches a certain critical mass, they begin a video worship experience, which eventually leads to the establishment of a regular weekend celebration.

The low-risk model allows CTK to experience rapid growth and powerful outreach.

The CTK team believes that the key to sustaining their approach is based on two factors:

1. Deliberate simplicity: the approach to developing ministry that allows for lower financial investment and higher dependence on volunteers.

2. Strong infrastructure: the development of web-based training resources and the securing of centralized-service staffing that is high quality, efficient, and effective.

Most Multi-Sites Are a Blend of Models

The ways that churches are employing the multi-site strategy vary as much as churches do. The approaches are not easy to categorize because most multi-site churches, especially larger congregations, are a blend of several models. Although we have chosen to confine our discussion to five broad models, these models are being tailored to fit local contexts in numerous ways.

Take Lake Pointe Church in greater Dallas, Texas, as an example. Its multi-site model includes a campus to its west and plans for campuses to its south, east, and north. In addition, it has a partnership with the state, which allowed the church to implement a low-risk site in an area prison. It also has a Spanish-speaking venue and envisions using video to take advantage of many other niche opportunities that are consistent with its community and context.

North Point Community Church in Atlanta also represents a mixed model, with a strategy that includes multiple campuses, video venues, and in recent days, the addition of strategic partner churches that operate independently but carry the vision, values, programming model, and video teaching of North Point's original campus.

Deciding Which Model Is Best for You

The following list presents some of the defining questions that shape the multiplicity of local models. These questions will help you tailor your multi-site approach both to your church and to your community.

1. Will all worship services be at the same campus?
2. Will all worship services be in the same language?
3. Will all locations be designed to have a similar feel?
4. Will all worship services each week have the same teacher?
5. Will all worship services be in the same geographic area?
6. Does the church use small groups during the week as an integral part of its approach?
7. Will all campuses stay connected to the original campus?
8. Will off-site campuses receive the same caliber of funding as the original location?

Far More Than Multiple Services

When Seacoast was just beginning the multi-site journey, we (Geoff and staff) called a meeting of all the department leaders at the original campus to discuss what a new Seacoast campus should look like. We agreed that every campus should look exactly like the original campus. Our logic was simple: obviously the way we were already doing church must be the right way, all you need to do is look at how God had blessed our church. Fueled by too many caramel macchiatos and caffe lattes, we quickly came to the conclusion that Seacoast would become the "Starbucks of churches," with each campus nearly indistinguishable from the others.

Three years after that meeting, the only thing we have in common with Starbucks is that we have coffee at every campus. We have big campuses and little campuses; some are really young, some pretty old; we have edgy rock and roll, and we have laid-back acoustic worship. We discovered that many things that work well at a large church in a suburban beach community don't necessarily transfer to an inner-city college campus or a blue-collar neighborhood. While all our campuses have a common mission and common set of core values, we have "become all things to all people" so that we "may save some of them by whatever means are possible" (1 Cor. 9:22, GNT). Seacoast could be described as a teaching-team, regional-campus, low-risk, partnership, video-venue model.

The key to a successful transition to being a multi-site church isn't in picking the right model. The key is knowing what God has called your church to be and then adapting parts and pieces of the various models to fit your unique mission in the world. In the next chapter, we'll explore the process of deciding whether making the multi-site transition will work for your church.

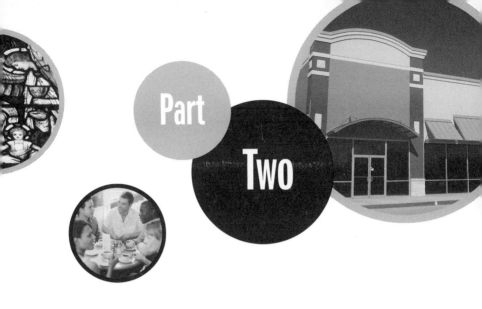

how to become

one church *in* many locations

Would It Work for You?

Consider why your church should explore multi-site as a strategy

> Go into all the world and preach the good news to all creation.
> — MARK 16:15

Pastor Jim Downing asked members of First United Methodist Church in Sedalia, Missouri, a long-established rural congregation, to open their wallets and purses and take out pictures of their children and grandchildren. The congregation happily showed the photos to others in the room.

"Does everyone in these pictures go to church? Do they all have an active faith in Jesus Christ?" the pastor probed. The mood in the room changed. Many shook their heads no.

"What would you do," he continued, "if a church in the town where *they* lived would actually reach out to them and provide a place for them to say yes to life, to love, and to God?"

The congregation overwhelmingly agreed, "We'd do almost anything to see that happen."

The pastor now had both their interest and their hearts. "I believe there are Christians in other cities, whose children or grandchildren have moved to *this* area, who are praying for a church here in Sedalia to do the same thing—to reach out to their loved ones. What if God is calling us to be that church?"

So began the decision of an old but growing congregation, with its facility one block off the county courthouse square, to add a second campus 2.7 miles away. There are only thirty thousand people in the entire county, but the church caught a vision for their seven thousand friends and neighbors who do not attend any church. With a say-yes attitude, the congregation determined to create a new campus with the understanding that it's for someone else.

From those 1997 discussions, when annual attendance averaged 136, it was a bold step for the congregation to open a new campus in 1999. Today, combining both sites, more than 750 people worship with First Church. Almost 300 of the newest attendees have now professed faith in Jesus Christ. And more than 350 people are weekly serving in a ministry area that fits them. The growth does not surprise Jim Downing, who affirms, "There is a whole community around us without Christ."

The church, who named its website www.firstsayyes.com to symbolize its stay-and-go attitude, is now extending its say-yes approach by adding a third site in Green Ridge, a town of five hundred people about fifteen miles away.

Multi-Site Solves Problems and Seizes Opportunities

What about *your* church? What is the need, problem, or opportunity that multi-site might solve for you? Are you facing a challenge? Are new opportunities surfacing that you want to take advantage of? Then read on. This chapter highlights why going multi-site has worked for others and why it might just be an answer for your church.

For Dave Ferguson, pastor of Community Christian Church in Chicago, each new campus represents an answer to a different problem. He wrote an article titled "The Multi-Site Church" for *Leadership Journal*[1] that explained how a multi-site church capitalizes on what Jim Collins, author of *Built to Last*, calls "the genius of the *and*"[2]—the paradoxical view that allows you to pursue both A and B simultaneously. Dave listed eight such advantages, each of which solves a problem in its own way:

- Grow larger *and* grow smaller
- Brand-new *and* trusted brand
- Staff with generalists *and* specialists
- Less cost *and* greater impact
- New-church vibe *and* big-church punch
- Move there *and* stay here
- More need *and* more support
- More outreach *and* more maturity

The various campuses of Community Christian Church embody the "genius of the *and*." In an incredibly fresh and eclectic manner, the church is reaching people throughout the Chicago area by employing different components of the models introduced in the previous chapter to address the specific needs of each target area. At the heart of their work is "The Big Idea," their version of the teaching-team model. Since the inception of the church, when five college buddies launched on a grand adventure, Community Christian has been committed to a teaching team that finds its expression in each campus and venue. This model has allowed for consistent, quality teaching across their community at all stages of their growth.

Community Christian also employs the partnership model. Their south campus, twelve miles away in Romeoville, was developed in partnership with a local development company. A man named Bruno Bottarelli approached Dave with a problem that Dave quickly saw as an opportunity. As a new believer, Bruno was passionate about his faith and committed to finding a way to integrate that faith with his vocation, real-estate development. So as he launched his next real-estate deal, it seemed perfectly natural to go to his pastor and ask him to be involved. Bruno was especially touched by the genuine sense of community he had been experiencing in a home-based small group. Bruno asked his pastor, "How can we get this kind of genuine community into the real-estate communities we build and manage?"

Believing in the "genius of the *and*," Dave replied, "Sure, let's see what might happen." The answer was to take the church to them. That was 1998. Today Highpoint Friendship Centre houses Community

Christian's Romeoville campus, where some one thousand people gather to worship each weekend. The church holds a long-term lease agreement to provide various types of programs within that facility, including programs directly tied to the church. (The partnership includes a for-profit organization called Institute for Community [www.instituteforcommunity.org] set up by Community Christian Church and the development company.)

Other Community Christian campuses use the video-venue model. Some are located in schools, others in community centers, and still others in transitioned church facilities. Every week at these video venues, one of two video teaching products is offered. The first is a videocast of the teaching recorded on Saturday night at a Community Christian location. The other video teaching product is a short film (twenty to twenty-five minutes) that is produced on location each week, featuring a teaching pastor on that week's Big Idea.

Community Christian has launched other sites in area high schools (another example of a low-risk model) and in a magnet school reaching the primarily Hispanic community in the Pilsen area of Chicago. This latter launch extends Community Christian's reach through the regional-campus model. Dave has said, "I used to lay awake at night thinking about how we would be able to afford to build a facility big enough for our vision and growth. Now I lay awake at night wondering, 'Which of the "Sunday morning empty boxes" will God open the doors on for our next campus?'"

Each of Community Christian's new campuses has addressed the church's ongoing challenge of creating more space. In each case, a both/and opportunity has been seized. And in each case, a new campus has advanced the work of Community Christian's mission of "helping people find their way back to God."

Measuring the Risks and Evaluating Opportunities

So will multi-site work for *your* church? You will need to take some time to prayerfully measure the risks and evaluate the opportunities of your situation.

All churches doing multi-site seem to have a comfort zone that surrounds the basic conviction that there are lots of ways to do it. The bigger divergence is in the level of risk that churches are willing to take.

What's Your Risk Level?

Becoming multi-site changes, and presumably enhances, who you are as a church ("We have a commitment to X; how does multi-site enhance X?"). It adds value to your church and to the people you're reaching. Sometimes it helps free up certain resources and recovers certain values lost along the way, such as a corporate sense of intimate community. But it also increases certain risk levels.

In assessing how much risk to take when spinning off multiple campuses, the self-diagnostic questions that churches tend to ask themselves include:

- How far are we willing to extend ourselves? To other rooms on our campus? Across town? Across our state or province? Around the world?
- How different will the satellites be from the original campus?
- How much unity of vision is required? Is this a branch, a franchise, or a licensee?
- How will the satellite sites connect back to the original campus?
- How centralized will we be?
- How much permission will we grant an off-site to fail?
- How much control will the original campus maintain?
- How much change will we allow in the way things are done at the original campus?
- How much momentum should we expect to see to determine if a new site is viable?
- How soon do we expect the extension campuses to move from being a resource drain to being a fully contributing resource?
- How many people (leaders and artists) need to be in place before we launch a new site?
- How will we prevent a loss of quality in the new site, and what is the defining point for deciding that the quality level is not acceptable?
- How much money will it take to birth the new site, both for the launch stage and to fund it until it reaches a point of self-support?

An advertisement for Electronic Data Systems shows a group of skilled workers building an airplane as it is flying, with one of them emphasizing, "We've got to get this airplane completed before we land!" That describes the approach of some church leaders. Other leaders don't want to launch without a well-mapped plan, from finances to staffing. The risk-takers, however, affirm that multi-site is an ever-moving target: "It's a process thing; we're moving toward it, and we need to keep at it."

Is Multi-Site Largely a White, Suburban, Middle-Class Deal?

Since most North Americans live in suburban areas, that's where most churches are too, including multi-site congregations. But rural churches can be multi-site, as the Sedalia example in this chapter shows.

What about ethnic or urban churches? You'll find examples of ethnic and urban multi-site churches throughout this book, including Eastern Star Church in Indianapolis (see chapter 2); National Community Church in Washington D.C., with two sites in the downtown area (see chapter 5); New Song Los Angeles, with a largely Asian first site and a largely African-American second site (see chapter 9); Eddie Long's New Birth Missionary Baptist Church in Georgia and North Carolina, with all three sites largely African American (see chapter 9); New Life Community Church in Chicago, with eight sites in Chicago proper, two of which use the Spanish language (see chapters 6 and 11); and Mosaic in Los Angeles, with four sites and seven gatherings in the LA area, all multiethnic (see preface).

We're 200 People — Can We Be Multi-Site?

The majority of churches in America have a weekly worship attendance of 200 or less people (adults and children). Are such churches involved in multi-site ministry? Is it a good idea?

The answer is yes, if you can answer in the affirmative to the three crucial questions at the end of this chapter. Churches of 200 people find it easiest to follow the low-risk model, the partnership model, and the regional-campus model, all localized to their areas. The most common outcome is services they take somewhere (to an assisted-living complex, a public park, etc.). Or they start new services, such as a weekend evening service, sometimes in more neutral locations, like a school or community center. Or they follow the mini-regional model like Southside in Surrey, British Columbia (chapter 4). Or they become sites of larger churches, as in the stories about New Life in Chicago (chapter 1), Windermere in Orlando (chapter 4), RockPointe in Calgary (chapter 7), or Lake Pointe in Texas (chapters 2, 5, and 7).

What's the Difference between Expanding to Multi-Site and Planting a New Church?

Many churches ask what the difference is between creating a new campus (also known as a branch campus or satellite) and launching a totally separate, new church (also known as church planting). As stated in the opening chapter, the idea of one church in multiple locations means you share "a common vision, budget, leadership, and board." If your new campus has a vision, budget, leader, or board that's not part of the sending campus, then you've started a new church or a mission campus, not a multi-site campus.

Why do some churches choose to become multi-site rather than to spin off new churches? Here are the advantages of being part of a multi-site church:

- Accountability
- Sharing of resources (stewardship)
- Infusion of trained workers
- Shared DNA (vision and core values)
- Greater prayer support
- Preestablished network for problem solving
- Not needing to "reinvent the wheel"
- Connection with others doing the same thing

Could multi-site also be a church-planting model? Absolutely. Many churches are doing just that, such as New Hope Christian Fellowship in Honolulu, Hawaii, pastored by Wayne Cordeiro. In 2000, New Hope began its first off-site video venue, inviting church families by zip code to attend a new campus three miles away. This opened up room at the 1,200-seat high school auditorium that the church rented for worship services. New Hope had filled the auditorium for five services as well as an 800-seat overflow tent, where worshipers view the service on a nine-by-twelve-foot LED screen.

Conditions for Consideration

Andy Calhoun serves as CEO of the Greater Charlotte YMCA. In that role, he oversees 7,000 volunteers, who serve over 250,000 people through eighteen branches in this rapidly growing area of North Carolina. Andy's passion for Christ and his effective leadership of a multi-unit nonprofit organization make him uniquely qualified to provide perspective on the multi-site church movement.

In a conversation with Andy, I (Geoff) asked him how the YMCA made decisions about launching new branches. He indicated that it was a great question because at any one point in time, they are considering eight to ten new ideas, and each idea (new location) has a champion who is very excited about the prospect. So when Andy faces a decision about expanding the ministry of the YMCA in Charlotte, he doesn't do so in a vacuum. He and his team review a well-prepared document called the "conditions for consideration." This document consists of a series of questions that help them discover and address the potential challenges in the proposed scenario.

Once a proposed site meets the conditions for consideration, a more thorough analysis of data occurs, including thorough market research, projected start-up costs, and fund-raising potential. Additional demographic data, provided by board members' companies (grocery stores, banks, etc.) give a complete picture of the target community. In addition to the calculable statistics, anecdotal information that portrays the passion of the regional and local leadership is key in making an effective decision.

Even with the same procedure surrounding each new launch, there is no sense of a cookie-cutter approach. "There is a saying around our organization," Andy says, "that when you open one YMCA, you open *one* YMCA." This maxim reminds everyone that when it comes to a new YMCA (as with a satellite campus of a church), there is no such thing as a generic, one-size-fits-all model.

Some people at New Hope were initially reluctant to try the off-site campus, but within a year, says Wayne, "it became so popular that we moved to two Sunday services. Within the next three years, we began video venues in seven off-site locations."

Each location, marked by a group of leaders who have pioneer hearts and the skills to lead, offers on-site worship, Sunday school, youth ministries, and a host of small group opportunities. One location is wired so that people can experience the message broadcast from the high school campus in real time, and the others view it by watching a just-delivered DVD.

For Wayne, the satellite breakouts are a church-planting plan. "Our goal for satellites is not necessarily to add locations. It is to develop new leaders. It is to edge these emerging leaders into their own teaching, where one day we can release them as stand-alone churches," he says. "When young leaders go out with this model, they have time to build relationships, develop teams, think about evangelism projects, do community outreach, and build leaders."

This church-planting model is designed so that the campus pastors do only about 10 percent of the weekend preaching during the first year. "Their main pulpit is the midweek services, where they build leaders and strengthen the core," Wayne explains. "So they are teaching every week, but the bar is not as high for the midweek teaching. It is mostly leadership training and biblical discipleship."

Over the next year, the campus pastors notch up to handling 40 percent of the weekend preaching. During year two, it goes up to about 60 percent. In their third year, they can still use the DVDs but no more than 30 percent of the time. By the fourth year, they may use the DVDs only on special occasions.

Three Crucial Questions about Timing

So we're back to the original question, "Would it work for you?" Expanding your church from one location to two or more is a move that has a great deal of potential but also tremendous risks. While the key criteria is, "What is God saying for your church in your community?" we've found that the following three questions often determine the success or failure of a church that is launching a new location.

The decision makers in your congregation need to sort through these crucial issues.

1. *How healthy is your church?* Is your church growing? Is it a great gathering place for people to find their way to God, to be discipled, and to find a place of ministry? Are the members of your church excited about bringing family and friends? Launching a second site will not bring health to an ailing congregation; and frankly it's generally not a good idea for an unhealthy church to reproduce itself. If you're unhealthy, why export your disease? One great way to check the health of your church is to take the Natural Church Development assessment (available at www.ncd-international.org/public/profiles.html).

2. *Is there a driving impetus behind your desire to go multi-site?* All of the leaders we've talked with at successful multi-site churches chose to open a second site because they saw no better option for fulfilling God's purpose for their church. At some churches, the building was packed, they had run out of viable service times, and building a larger facility didn't seem to be the answer. At other churches, there was a sense of mission to go into the next city, into the next county, or across a cultural chasm they had been unable to cross. At still other churches, the congregation had a strong desire to take the ministry of their church into the neighborhoods of the members. In each case, though, multi-site was not seen as merely another program or strategy but rather as a key component in fulfilling their God-inspired vision. Starting a second site without a compelling drive behind it is like trying to give birth without being pregnant.

3. *Are the key leaders behind the decision?* Going multi-site can stretch the budget, invite criticism from other churches, and make new demands on church leadership; therefore, to be successful, it is vital that the key leaders of the church be unified and enthusiastic about the decision to go multi-site. While it is difficult to get 100 percent buy-in when moving in a new direction, if the senior leadership is not sold on the concept of being a church with multiple locations, it should be a major warning light.

Now Our Critics Think We're Cool

Seacoast never intended to become a multi-site church. In 2001, we (Geoff) were averaging 3,500 people in three weekend services, and we were in the process of building a 4,000-seat auditorium. Then we ran into a brick wall of resistance from neighbors whose slogan became "Not in my backyard." The debate became front-page news under the headline "Seacoast Plans Building Twice the Size of Wal-Mart." (In our community, being compared to Wal-Mart is a major insult.)

The issue finally came to a head at a meeting before the town council. Senior pastor Greg Surratt (my older brother) delivered a beautiful speech that night. He appealed to God, to country, to apple pie, and all that is good in America. He referred to our city's nickname, the Holy City, where no building can be taller than the tallest church steeple. He reminisced about a time when cities were built around churches rather than churches being shut out by cities. He finished with a heartfelt plea for the council members to stand up and do the right thing. The council was so moved that they soundly voted us down!

"I went home, drew the blinds, and put on some country music," Greg later told us. "I didn't know what to do. 'Not in my backyard' had transformed the way we do church. We couldn't grow more in our current location, and those who opposed us were the target of our ministry—exactly the kind of people God had called us to reach."

Greg had heard about churches who were experimenting with video-cast to do church in more than one location. He grabbed a friend, Byron Davis, and they did a whirlwind weekend of visits to some of these churches. They flew to San Diego to experience a Saturday night service at North Coast Church. They flew overnight to catch the Sunday morning service at Heartland Community Church in Rockford, Illinois, which shows videos from Willow Creek rather than having their own teaching pastor; lead pastor Doug Thiesen says his gift is music, not preaching. As soon as the service was over, they drove to Wheaton, Illinois, to experience Willow Creek's first regional ministry center. "At the end of the trip, Byron and I both agreed that it just might work," Greg says. "After all, what did we have to lose?"

Fast-forward three years, and we had grown from 3,500 to 7,000 people in weekend services without adding a single building. On Easter

2005, almost 11,000 people attended our twenty-three services across nine locations.

One day Greg ran into the leader of our opposition on the town council. "The man stuck his hand out and said, 'Greg, we are so proud of you and your church. Don't you think God somehow used us in a small way to propel you into the future?'

Several thoughts came to mind, like, "Yes, God also spoke to donkeys in Bible times" or "Yes, feeding Christians to the lions in Nero's time also helped spread the Christian faith," or "Yes, but your picture isn't going in our foyer."

Instead, Greg reports, "I didn't say any of those things. I shook his hand and mumbled something about God's love for everyone. As I walked away, though, I realized that now our critics think what we're doing is cool."

• •

Workout

So what about it? Is multi-site right for *your* church? In this workout, we help you tackle the question, "Should our church go multi-site?" So limber up, take a couple of deep breaths, and tackle your first workout. If you decide the answer is yes, you should go multi-site, we'll see you in "On a Mission from God" (chapter 4), in which we'll look at the factors that have led churches to successfully pursue a multi-site strategy. If you decide the answer is no, multi-site isn't for your church, thanks for buying the book; you're helping put our kids through college. But plan to pick up the book in a year or two to revisit the idea of becoming multi-site.

Should *Your* Church Go Multi-Site? (A Self-Diagnostic Tool)

video venues on-site · extension sites · multiple campuses · satellite ministries · alternative worship service in the church gym · concurrent worship· off-site video-café congregations · taking responsibility for a struggling congregation · additional service in nursing home or fire station · other variations

How can your congregation know if a multi-site approach is right for you? This self-diagnostic tool should help you gain insight.

Directions.

For each statement, rate yourself:

0 = Not applicable or disagree
1 = Marginally agree
2 = Somewhat agree
3 = Agree
4 = Strongly agree

Clarity of Call

_____ 1. The multi-site approach is an idea we're already praying about, talking about, or doing.

_____ 2. As we earnestly pray, we are becoming convinced that multi-site is the type of approach God wants us to explore.

_____ 3. Becoming multi-site seems to be a natural extension of our church's mission or vision.

_____ 4. We sensed God's affirmation when we previously experimented with a new location or venue.

_____ 5. We cannot accomplish all God has called us to do and be without becoming multi-site.

_____ 6. There is widespread and prayerful agreement that now is the time to launch a new site or venue.

Motivation

_____ 1. Due to our recent growth, we feel we *must* initiate some type of expansion.

_____ 2. We're facing an opportunity that could become a ready bridge to a multi-site extension.

_____ 3. We're strongly drawn to the idea, typically embodied in multi-site settings, of getting bigger by becoming smaller.

Receptive Audience

_____ 1. We know of specific people we could reach if we brought "church" closer to their location, style, or language.

_____ 2. Everything we've experienced to date tells us that if we launch a new site or venue, people will come.

_____ 3. If we launch a new site or venue, the people of our church seem very likely both to come and to invite their friends.

Leadership

_____ 1. If we send our best leaders to the new site or venue, other leaders in the wings will quickly step in to fill the gaps.

_____ 2. Leadership development is a value already deeply ingrained in our church culture.

_____ 3. Our present leadership team is willing to devote the time and energy needed to mentor and coach a new set of leaders.

Know-How

_____ 1. We are visiting or studying multi-site churches or are developing a mentor-church relationship with one.

_____ 2. We've done other ministries in the past that have parallels to multi-site.

_____ 3. We could handle the technology or communications issues associated with becoming multi-site.

Relationship Strengths

_____ 1. Our church leadership team currently has excellent credibility with the congregation.

_____ 2. Our leadership team has been stable enough lately that we could make some changes without rattling the congregation too much.

_____ 3. I can envision a strong pastor-people unity, joy, and prayer support when we launch a new site or venue.

Finances

_____ 1. Our debt load as a church is quite manageable (or nonexistent).

_____ 2. Our people would give generously for a onetime offering to help with start-up costs.

_____ 3. Our general fund could provide up to two years of ongoing financial support for the new site or venue.

_____ 4. We have ideas about an available facility that we could afford.

_____ TOTAL (of 100 possible points)

The following ranges would compare with other churches around the country:

If your total is 25 points or less, your timing seems very premature. If you launch a new site anytime in the near future, you will probably lack the support, momentum, or other essential elements that could give staying power to your multi-site endeavor.

If your total is 26 – 50 points, you have potential but are probably not ready to go multi-site. Continue to pray, explore, discuss, learn, and plan. Keep developing leaders so that you'll have enough leaders when the timing is right.

If your total is 51 – 75 points, you are close to being ready for a multi-site venture. Review your strengths and build on them. Examine your weak points and compensate for them as appropriate.

If your total is 76 – 100 points, you have a high likelihood of success compared to other churches that are doing multi-site.

Based on the results of this self-diagnostic tool, what do you need to do next? Indicate the steps you need to take and when you will take them.

1. _____

   _____

2. _____

   _____

3. _____

   _____

On a Mission from God

Discern God's call for your church and leadership

> "The Spirit of the Sovereign LORD is on me, because the LORD has anointed me to preach good news to the poor. He has sent me to bind up the brokenhearted, to proclaim freedom for the captives and release from darkness for the prisoners, to proclaim the year of the LORD's favor."
>
> — ISAIAH 61:1 - 2

In October 1993, Mark Brewer held a meeting to discuss his vision for a different type of church in the Denver metro area. Early the next year, Colorado Community Church was birthed, with its first services held at the Hyatt Regency. Early growth found the new church moving from hotel to high school to business complex and eventually to its first purchased facility in Cherry Hills Village.

By 1997, the expanding congregation was meeting in three Sunday services. Continuing growth led to a decision to develop multiple campuses in the metro area versus one centralized megachurch. The

Aurora section of Denver was targeted as the location for a second campus, and a goal of five campuses in ten years was established.

Up to this point, the Colorado Community story sounds much the same as that of many other growing churches who have met the challenges of a growing congregation by establishing multiple campuses. But the move to multi-site was more than a growth strategy for the Colorado Community team; they were on a mission from God to be an agent of community transformation.

Central to the development of their multi-site strategy is the call to be externally focused—to meet the needs of the city where God planted them a decade ago. When senior pastor Robert Gelinas describes their locations, he uses language like "mission posts" and "base camps"—sites around the city that exist for the purpose of serving others and ultimately for the purposes of the kingdom of God. The launch plan for new campuses is driven by discerning the intersection of the community's needs and the church's resources—the place where the Colorado Community team believes the greatest impact and transformation can occur.

Although the names change and the specifics differ, the story is much the same around the world, in places where leaders and churches are responding to God's call to be the church ... in many locations.

How Multi-Sites Get Started

Things looked pretty bleak for Israel. The Philistines were once again challenging King Saul and his army to battle, and the smart money was on the Philistines: "The Philistines assembled to fight Israel, with three thousand chariots, six thousand charioteers, and soldiers as numerous as the sand on the seashore" (1 Sam. 13:5).

Saul had started out with three thousand soldiers. They lacked chariots, but they did have a couple of guys who could make the sound of thundering horses by banging coconuts together. When they saw the odds against them, their number quickly dwindled to six hundred. To make matters worse, counting the swords of Saul and his son Jonathan, the army had a grand total of two weapons among them. (They didn't even have the coconut bangers; Geoff made them up.) Despite the overwhelming odds, Jonathan had a plan: he and his armor-bearer would take his half of the weapons cache and sneak up on the Philistine army. He had an interesting strategy: "Perhaps the LORD will act in our behalf. Nothing can hinder the LORD from saving, whether by many or by few" (1 Sam. 14:6).

Jonathan was right: God acted on their behalf. After Jonathan and his armor-bearer had killed twenty Philistines, panic spread through the enemy camp. The entire army jumped in their chariots and beat a path out of Micmash.

What would cause two men, armed only with a sword, to face thousands of enemies? They were on a mission for God.

What prompts a church to take a multi-site approach? We will examine several motivations for making the initial move, but all of the churches we have studied had one common denominator: they felt they were on a mission for God. They are willing to do whatever it takes to reach their towns, their communities, and their generation for the cause of Christ.

What Prompts a Church to Develop Multiple Venues or Locations?

1. Along-the-Way Addition

The majority of multi-site churches did not start with a founding-day intention to become multi-site. Some say they stumbled onto the idea along the way. Most were trying to solve a problem and made creative decisions that resulted in becoming a multi-site church.

According to surveys we've conducted through Leadership Network, the most-cited reason for launching multiple campuses or multiple venues is lack of space, ranging from a lack of seats or parking spots at optimal service times to zoning or building restrictions on future growth. The second most-cited reason is a vision to impact through "more" instead of "bigger" — a desire to avoid certain downsides of megachurches.

> Most were trying to solve a problem and made creative decisions that resulted in becoming a multi-site church.

Overcrowding. One of the easiest multi-site trigger points to identify is overcrowding. A typical example is First Baptist Church in Windermere, Florida, just outside Orlando. Its seating capacity was 500, and leaders felt their campus limits were constraining the church's growth. "We were out of space in a rapidly growing area and were unable to meet the demands of our community," says pastor Mark Matheson.

In 2000, they were contacted by another church based only two miles away with just the opposite problem. Sunday worship drew fewer than twenty people per week from the local community. After discussing the matter, both churches voted almost unanimously for the struggling church to become a satellite church of First Baptist. "The addition of this church gave us the vision for a multi-campus approach," Mark says. "We formed a multi-campus church organization—one church on two campuses—and gave our new congregation a full-time campus pastor." Using The Big Idea approach developed by Community Christian Church in Chicago (see pp. 36–37 and 46–48), the two campuses follow the same teaching themes about 75 percent of the time.[1]

The search for a solution to overcrowding continues at First Baptist. It is trying creative angles to get maximum usage from its present facilities, such as a worship service on Wednesday night that begins at 10:00 p.m. and ends about midnight. "Due to the tourist industry, Orlando never shuts down," Mark explains. "Sunday might as well be Wednesday around here." The Wednesday night service, launched in January 2003, was averaging more than 100 in attendance by the end of 2005.

First Baptist also launched a third campus in 2004 that members built on a fifty-one-acre site. This far more sizable property accommodates a 3,000-seat sanctuary, a bold initiative for a church running about 2,000 people across five services/venues at three sites at the end of 2005.

New group. The desire to reach a new area or target demographic is another trigger point that prompts a church to become multi-site. A good example is The Garden, a "nontraditional service" church that has met weekly since 1995 in Beef and Boards dinner theater in Indianapolis. The Garden calls itself a "blossom" (or satellite) outreach of fifty-year-old St. Luke's United Methodist Church in Indianapolis.

The Garden started when God led several leaders at St. Luke's to try to reach those people who do not have a church background, those who are unfamiliar with the liturgy, customs, and language of established religion and are uncomfortable in a traditional church setting, those who feel left out or disenfranchised by the church, and those who feel the church is irrelevant and disconnected from their lives.

A contemporary rock band provides music (mostly secular contemporary songs and contemporary Christian hits), supported by PowerPoint projected lyrics. There are no handbells, organ, or choir. There is no praise music or hymns, no passing of an offering plate, and no clerical garb for the pastor, Linda McCoy. Her spoken message is brief, about twelve minutes, and video clips are interspersed throughout the message, either original productions or clips from current movies. "And the tiered seating layout—tables of two, four, and eight—is a perfect venue to create little communities," adds creative director Suzanne Stark.

The Garden, maxed out by its three services, began looking for property of its own but decided to remain multi-site and to grow instead by planting. It found an available banquet hall named Oak Hill Mansion several miles north and began a service there, sending the sermon live via T1 video line. Through a sense of partnership, Oak Hill became rent-free for the church in 2004.[2]

Need meeting opportunity. Other churches become multi-site when they face an opportunity that matches their mission. Healing Place Church in Baton Rouge, Louisiana, is built on the mission "to be a healing place for a hurting world." Pastors Dino and DeLynn Rizzo and the staff at the church have a passion to express Christ through creative means while expressing his love in practical ways. Community outreaches and missions projects of every kind are just a couple of the ways that the gospel of Jesus Christ is shared with countless individuals.

In 2004, Healing Place held its first services in the Donaldsonville area of Baton Rouge. This site, Dream Center Church, was planted as an outgrowth of the intersection of the mission of Healing Place and the opportunity to show the love of Jesus to one of the poorest communities in the state. Healing Place continues its passion to reach out to all kinds of people through its launch of a Spanish campus in the Ascension Parish area. The greater Baton Rouge area has a population of over 10,000 Spanish Americans, and Healing Place has connected with leaders in the local Spanish-speaking community to create another arm of the church.

Healing Place has now established five campuses, each in response to a specific opportunity to meet the needs of the poor, the oppressed, and the forgotten, as well as needs of the variety of cultures found in Baton Rouge.

Mission clarification. A final trigger point for going multi-site is an internal struggle with value alignment. The outcome can be a mission clarification and a decision to develop multiple campuses.

Southside Community Church in Surrey, British Columbia, developed an attitude of using multiple campuses to go to where the people are. In 1993, Cam and Shelley Roxburgh planted Southside in a very poor neighborhood. One of the key ingredients in Southside's launch was the fact that the members of the core group moved into the neighborhood. "This made all the difference," explains Cam. "The church grew very quickly and was soon packed out. Those who lived here did a great job with incarnational ministry, but the people coming from farther away had a hard time being incarnational with their neighbors."

The discovery prompted Cam to ask, "If God can do this in this neighborhood, why not in another neighborhood?"

So after starting an additional service, the leadership team decided to launch another congregation in a neighborhood where a key group of the church's core people were living. Southside's second site was launched in 1997. By the year 2000, both congregations had grown, and the time came to launch two new sites. By spring 2000, Southside had become one church with four congregations.

> For Southside, being multi-site is a necessary foundation for community transformation.

For Southside, being multi-site is a necessary foundation for community transformation. "From day one, it was about planting a church that would plant churches. Then it evolved into planting a church that would launch local congregations," Cam says.

2. From the Beginning

A few churches are planted with a "one church, many locations" approach in mind. "We didn't go multi-site because we were forced to," says Brent Knox, one of the founding pastors of Evergreen Community

Church in Minneapolis-St. Paul. "We took this path because it was our strategy from the beginning—going to wherever an evangelical presence is needed. The idea was as deeply rooted in our core values as were church planting, plurality of leadership, creating leadership teams, and having all the leaders of all the locations work together."

Evergreen was founded in 1988. Six years later (1994), it launched a second site. Three years later (1997), it birthed a third. Two years after that (1999) came the fourth site. Two years later (2001), Evergreen started a church in Berlin, Germany. Two years after that (2003) came the fifth Twin Cities location. These five sites house seven services/venues weekly, and as 2005 ended, their total weekly U.S. worship averaged 2,600. All U.S. locations come together for couples and singles conferences, Christmas Eve services, periodic all-location "superservices," and some leadership training.

> "We took this path because it was our strategy from the beginning."
> — Brent Knox

In the beginning, all Evergreen locations used rented school buildings. Services were held in the auditorium, and the nursery and Sunday school classes were in the lunchroom and classrooms. Two Evergreen locations now share church space with two other churches. Each site has a different teaching team, but they sometimes try to run a parallel track for worship and programming, such as featuring the same video or skit at all locations on a given weekend. Two times a year, they collaborate on the same teaching series.

Much good has come from having so many locations, especially keeping a priority on outreach. "We feel called to be strong in outreach," Brent says. "There are many churches in America that are great at teaching but not many that are good at outreach. We want to continue church-planting and to continue creating venues that reach out to specific people groups."

Always Outreach

The multi-site ride has most often been about opportunities—reaching more people with the gospel, developing more leaders, and influencing other churches. As we noted earlier, multi-site isn't a vision by itself but a vehicle to achieve the vision.

One day as my (Geoff's) grandfather, E. L. Surratt, was praying in the back of his little grocery store in Visalia, California, he felt God gave him a mission: he was to return to Oklahoma to start a church. E. L. had never pastored a church and had never preached a sermon. He had only a sixth-grade education. When E. L. left Oklahoma years before, he had a reputation as a mean man who sold moonshine and loved to fight. He had wounded a man in a gunfight, and the man had vowed to kill E. L. the next time he saw him. Returning to start a church might present some challenges, but E. L. was on a mission from God.

> Remember that multi-site isn't a vision by itself, but a vehicle to achieve the vision.

He sold the grocery store and his modest house, loaded up his family and all their possessions, and headed to the desolate plains of western Oklahoma. E. L. eventually stopped the car in front of an abandoned church building in a dusty wheat field in the middle of nowhere. He told his family that this was the building God had shown him that day in the back of the grocery store; this is where they would start a church. That Sunday, E. L. preached his first sermon to the new congregation of five: E. L., his wife, and their three children.

Life was tough, but they persevered. Children began coming to hear my grandmother tell Bible stories, and then they began to bring their parents. E. L. worked to fix up the old building, and within a few months, they had established a viable congregation in the wheat fields of Oklahoma. Eventually all of E. L.'s children (including my dad) and all of his grandchildren (including me) became pastors. Thousands of people have been impacted by my grandfather's life, but it began with a calling to a mission from God.

Every successful multi-site church we've encountered has felt a similar mission. These churches weren't looking for the latest church-growth strategy or a new ministry or project; they felt a compelling call from God to reach people. Just as my grandfather used that abandoned Oklahoma church building, going multi-site was simply a vehicle these churches used to help fulfill their calling.

● ●

What is the compelling mission of your church? Are the key leaders on board with that mission? Do they even know what your church's mission is? This workout will help your key leaders discover, define, and deliver the unique mission of your church in a multi-site environment. When you've completed the workout, grab a quick shower and join us in chapter 5, where we'll be looking at the incredible variety of opportunities that have led churches to begin their multi-site journey. One of those opportunities is most likely knocking at your church's door now.

Your church is on a mission from God that is different from that of any other church. The questions below will help you clarify that mission and examine how opening a new campus will help you fulfill what God has called you to.

Gather several of the key leaders of your church. Give each leader a copy of this workout and give everyone a chance to complete the questions on their own. Once everyone has had a chance to answer all the questions, go through the questions one at a time and write answers on a whiteboard or flip chart. Be sure to give everyone a chance to share before trying to arrive at a consensus for each question.

This workout is most effective when an outside, neutral party facilitates the discussion, when distractions are kept to a minimum, and when plenty of time is allotted to work out the problems.

Fulfilling Your God-Given Mission

1. What is the one-sentence purpose of our church?

    We exist to ... _____

    _____

    _____

    _____

    _____

    _____

2. What are the five core values of our church?

   a. _____

   b. _____

   c. _____

   d. _____

   e. _____

3. What unique, specific mission has God called our church to accomplish?

   _____

   _____

4. What sets our church apart from all the other churches in our community?

   _____

   _____

5. What seemingly insurmountable obstacles does our church currently face?

   _____

   _____

6. What outstanding opportunities are ripe for our church to pick?

   _____

   _____

7. What is the one compelling thing that drives the key leaders of our church?

_____

_____

8. How will opening a second campus impact the answers to the preceding questions?

_____

_____

Opportunity Knocks

Don't expect "We've always done it this way" to become your church motto

> "Here I am! I stand at the door and knock. If anyone hears my voice and opens the door, I will come in and eat with him, and he with me." — REVELATION 3:20

What do the largest nightclub in Washington D.C., a coffeehouse on Capitol Hill, and the movie-theater complex at Union Station have in common? According to Pastor Mark Batterson, "They make great sanctuaries for worshiping God." All three spaces are being spiritually redeemed by National Community Church, where Mark is lead pastor. "We're practicing orthodox Christianity in some unorthodox places," Mark says.

Mark has nothing against more traditional church buildings. In fact, when he and a small core team started the interdenominational National Community Church in 1996, they followed the common pattern of initially renting space (a public school) with dreams of eventually buying property and a facility of their own.

Then eleven months after its launch, through no fault of its own, the congregation became nomadic. The flock of fewer than fifty had to find a new place to meet, so they experimented with meeting in a movie-theater complex. "Union Station wasn't plan A," Mark comments.

Within a few weeks, however, Mark and the growing congregation had a different perspective. "Union Station is the most visited destination in the nation's capital," he says. "We've got our own subway stop, bus stop, train stop, and parking garage. We've got forty food-court restaurants right outside our meeting site. The theaters give us multiple meeting rooms with comfortable seats and screens that function as modern-day stained glass, comparable to how medieval churches used pictures to tell the gospel story. What more accessible and visible location could we want? I can't imagine a better beachhead for reaching the unchurched and dechurched in D.C."

The church even plays with its setting, such as using popcorn boxes to receive the offering. But the location does more than add fun to worship, prayer, preaching, and receiving Holy Communion in a place used for entertainment the rest of the week; it removes an obstacle for anyone intimidated or threatened by a church building. "Our congregation is 75 percent unchurched; 80 percent are single, and 80 percent are twenty-somethings. Those demographics scream for a place like theaters and commuter stops," Mark says.

Today Mark is not content to go to only one theater complex, one nightclub, and one coffee shop. He is convinced that the church belongs in the middle of the marketplace, so the more places it goes, the better. "I love the idea of doing church in the marketplace," he says. What better place to 'contend for the faith' (Jude 3) or to look for people in the highways and byways and 'compel them to come in' (Luke 14:23 NKJV)! In fact, our identity and vision is now to meet in theaters near Metro stops throughout the D.C. area."

> "We learned that you don't need a building or 1,000 people to go multi-site."
> — Mark Batterson

Mark's expanded vision came in a dramatic moment as he was doing a personal prayer walk. Mark looked at a large Metro map display and envisioned a church meeting at or near each stop. "It was a Damascus Road experience," he says. Within a few months, the church sent out 75 of its then 500 people to launch a second location at Ballston Common Mall.

"We learned that you don't need a building or 1,000 people to go multi-site," Mark says. So as the church grows—from an initial 19 in 1996 to 50 in 2000, 350 in 2001, 500 in 2002, 700 in 2003, 800 in 2004, and more than 1,000 by 2006—Mark plans to open sites in each Metro stop area where people from the church have relational connections.

People Who Heard an Opportunity Knocking

A major theme of this book is that no single model dominates the multi-site horizon. Within churches of every model, one or more individuals have eyes of faith to spot an opportunity. Then within a permission-giving culture, the opportunity becomes a reality. Here are the stories of four more individuals who spotted an opportunity, with many new lives being touched for Jesus Christ as a result.

Multiple-Choice Church

In 1998, Chris Mavity joined the staff of North Coast Church, an Evangelical Free congregation in Vista, California. He had previously served on the staff of a fast-growing congregation and looked forward to serving as small groups director under Larry Osborne, lead pastor at North Coast.

The church was housed in a retail-industrial warehouse complex. The layout offered the church plenty of room for growth, but only as side-by-side units with separate outside entrances. One unit housed the children's ministry, and another the youth ministry. The largest unit had become the church's 500-plus-seat auditorium. As the church continued to reach out and grow, it kept adding new services in that auditorium, reaching a total of four services, two on Saturday nights and two on Sunday mornings. Larry had developed a preaching team but found that having two Saturday night services turned the weekend into an emotionally draining marathon. Time with his family was being squeezed out, and he began to dread the weekends. "We couldn't find any other good available time slots, our volunteer pool was already stretched thin, and our teaching team was running out of emotional energy," he says.

Then Larry nearly passed out during one of his sermons. In the weeks that followed, Larry had another dizzy spell during a Sunday

> No single model dominates the multi-site horizon.

morning message and again the next day while driving. Worried that it might happen again while he was on stage, Larry began to experience the symptoms of a panic attack most weekends. At that point, worried about Larry's long-term health, the church board decreed there would be no fifth weekend service.

Without the option of adding additional services, Larry decided to provide a different kind of overflow room, one that would be a reward rather than a punishment for latecomers. By using live worship, providing Starbucks coffee, adding some incentive elements, and putting only the teaching on the screen, he hoped that he could turn a typically negative experience into a positive one for those who could not find room in the main service.

"I've always said that it's leaders who like it big, but most people like it small," says Larry. "I figured we could find a way to create a small-church atmosphere with all the programs and amenities of a large church."

Larry then asked Chris to develop the vision and make it happen. But as Chris talked and prayed about the dilemma, he became convinced that it could and should go much further than Larry's dream of an overflow room that was a reward, not a punishment. Chris believed he could turn it into an actual siphon, a service with such a strong reward element that people would choose to go to it rather than to the main service. He believed he could achieve this by focusing on the quality of the ambiance and worship while building a team of people who looked on the new venue as their special ministry.

The first weekend attendance at the video café was 173 in September 1998. Three years later, 2,300 adults were choosing video venues for worship. As new venues were added, each one was targeted at a mindset rather than at an age group. The reward factor was linked to the targeted audience — one venue offers Starbucks coffee, another Mountain Dew soft drinks, and another Krispy Kreme doughnuts. More important, each worship venue offers its own distinctive style of live worship and an ambiance unique to the target audience. One venue called Traditions features hymns and a more sedate color scheme, while The Edge has huge subwoofers and urban art.

The element unifying all of the venues is the message, which is shown by videocast in all of the on-site and off-site venues. In addition, the venues and sites are tied together by a small group ministry that is sermon based, using a lecture-lab approach to discuss the principles and application of the previous week's sermon. Within several years, almost two-thirds of the congregation preferred the video venues over the services in the larger auditorium, where the preaching was live. The attendance grew to more than 6,000 people on the initial campus and satellite campuses, yet for most people, it had the feel of a church of only 500–800 people.

Many churches experiment first with going to new locations and then try to reach various lifestyles represented at that new location. North Coast did the lifestyle focus first, but now it too has expanded to multiple locations—five different campuses at present within a twenty-mile area.[1]

North Coast Church is an example of spotting opportunity through video venues, and Chris Mavity is now the executive director of North Coast Training Network, designed to train leaders for new North Coast sites, as well as the many leaders from other churches who come to learn from North Coast.

Fire-Station Church

North Little Rock fireman Jeff West attended an equipping class about taking his faith to his community and workplace. The class was taught at his church, Fellowship Bible Church of Little Rock, Arkansas.

Jeff's mind went immediately to the community he knew best: firefighters. "What about fire stations?" he thought, aware that a lot of firefighters are stuck at their firehouses on Sundays. Jeff also knew that his church would soon be opening a video venue on campus. "Why couldn't we do the same thing in our firehouses?" he asked himself.

A short time later, while riding the parking shuttle at church, Jeff met Phil Pounder. He learned that Phil is not only a fellow firefighter, but also a fire chief in the Little Rock fire department. They got talking about various possibilities. Then they and others together approached the leadership team of Fellowship Bible Church with their idea.

The outcome was simple but highly effective. It was reproducible in any number of fire stations. The church would give them a DVD copy of each sermon, the note-taking outline from the bulletin, and a brochure that introduces the current sermon series. Each of these was already available for anyone. The only adaptation made was to add a firehouse-edition personalized look to the DVD.

Phil became the host at his firehouse — starting the service, playing the DVD, and facilitating an after-sermon discussion. The idea has been well received, leading to multiple fire-station sites, each with a local host. In 2004, five different fire stations participated; in 2005, up to twenty fire stations participated.

Why use teaching from Fellowship Bible Church rather than tuning in to a national-caliber television preacher? "Use of our own teaching becomes a connecting point to attract people into the life of our church body," says Craig Cheney, the church's worship-venue overseer. "It strengthens a relationship that's already in place. They know something about us, and in many cases, we've served them as a church and invited them to our church through a variety of methods over recent years." The next natural step is to connect the members of the fire company with one of Fellowship Bible's small groups.

The church's leadership development is framed around relationships, and the outreach follows that same relational pattern. As Craig says, "Without the relationship, we're just bringing them a program. Programs don't produce life change. God uses people in relationship to each other to bring about life change. And life change is what it's all about. What started as one man's desire to be nurtured personally became a vision to reach many, with discovery of a practical way to do that."

The fire-station venues are an example of spotting opportunity through a low-risk model.

Shopping-Center Church

Who could imagine that a cultural center located at the center of City Place — West Palm Beach's most popular outdoor shopping area — could become a house of worship? Ironically, what is now known as the Harriet Himmel Theater was once a church building before it became, as one newspaper describes it, a "Disneyfied clock tower, concert hall, and high school prom venue." But today the old 1920s church has been transformed back into, of all things, a church.

People have fun noting that churchgoers can use the mall's valet service. And given the proximity of all the high-end stores and nice restaurants, locals may jokingly tease about the church, "Does it take reservations?" and "What's the return policy?" and "There's nothing eternal at City Place, except for the wait at the Cheesecake Factory!"

But Tom Mullins, founding pastor of Christ Fellowship Church in Palm Beach Gardens, Florida, saw an opportunity to reach the college and young-adult crowd. Christ Fellowship started in 1984 as a Bible study in the Mullins' home. Tom then led its growth to 4,000 people on a four-acre site. The church moved to a larger campus and grew further to about 9,000 people.

Additional growth seemed too challenging at that site, so in 2004, Christ Fellowship opened a campus twenty miles away in Wellington, Florida. Using a middle school, Christ Fellowship Wellington offers a complete parallel to the original Palm Beach Gardens campus: stellar children's ministries, strong student programs, and live worship with a popular worship leader from the Palm Beach Gardens campus. Sermons are videocasts, facilitated by a campus pastor. The instant campus serves about 1,500 people weekly, many of whom are involved in weekday home-based small groups as well.

Now the church has done the same thing at its third site: Christ Fellowship City Place. The starting point is called Ascent, a college and young-adult worship experience Sundays at 11:11 a.m., which went to two services in August 2005. A month later, a third service was added for the parents and grandparents.

As at Christ Fellowship Wellington, most of the preaching comes as video from the Palm Beach Gardens campus. Many young adults have been reached who likely would not have come to the Palm Beach Gardens campus. Just as important, a sizable group of young-adult members have moved from the bleachers to a meaningful role in ministry as they lead the City Place outreach.

Why not start new churches instead of becoming multi-site? "The traditional plan has been to make each church independent, letting it sink or swim," Tom says. "Our model is to support each other, stay focused in purpose and mission, yet allow different campuses to have unique expressions."

Christ Fellowship, including its shopping-center church, is an example of spotting opportunity through a regional-campus model.

Lend-a-Pastor Church

Since the 1978 arrival of Ed Young Sr. as pastor, Second Baptist Church in Houston, Texas, has grown from a weekly attendance of 350 to over 20,000 each Sunday. By 1990, it was the fourth-largest Protestant church in America, with the country's largest singles ministry. Under its dynamic pastor, life at the church campus seemed like one never-ending building program.

When it ran out of space in the 1990s, the church made a bold move: it would open a second campus fifteen miles to the west. Ed, a popular preacher with a widely known broadcast ministry, shuttled between the two campuses to do as much of the preaching as possible.

Then a struggling church on the north side of Houston asked for help. Second Baptist sent one of its leading staff pastors to help bring health back to the indebted and troubled church, which voted to merge with Second Baptist. He also helped instill the DNA of Second Baptist in the church. Over several years, the two Baptist cultures became one, though there were many rough spots—for example, different understandings of what a deacon is to do. "Merging is not the melting together of two cultures but the absorbing of one culture into another," Ed says. "It very rarely results in the new entity becoming the best of both organizations. Instead, it almost always involves the loss of one culture and the expansion of another. In adding other sites, the ultimate desire is to reproduce the life and culture of the original church in another area and enhance the effectiveness of a church system that is elsewhere firing on all cylinders."

The loan-a-pastor approach ultimately worked for the north campus, but it also had an unexpected consequence for the other campuses. As Second Baptist spotted more opportunities to start new campuses, the most recent ones in movie theaters starting in January 2006, it realized that even with the "branding" attraction of Ed Young Sr., a broader preaching team was needed.

Today Doug Paige preaches regularly at the Second Baptist North campus. The original Woodway campus and West campus have a mix of preaching by Ed Young Sr. and Ben Young, one of Ed's sons, some in person and some via videocast.

Additional new locations are all anticipated to have campus pastors and teaching via videocast. Some might initially think that Ed Young "is" Second Baptist. But that one-man image is not at all the whole story. He is not only an incredible up-front personality; he is also a great mentor of others.

"To go multi-site, a church's leader must be able to reproduce the passion, systems, and culture of the current site in the lives of others —others who in turn will lead at the new campuses," Ed says.

Second Baptist is a model of a church that spotted opportunity through a teaching-team model.

Opportunities for Churches of Every Size

The first decade of this century will be remembered for the many high-visibility churches that expanded to multiple venues and campuses. Media attention has been constant as Chicago's Willow Creek launched its first regional campus in 2001 and its fourth in 2005; Atlanta's North Point moved into its second on-campus auditorium in 2001 and its Buckhead campus in 2003; Saddleback near Los Angeles began offering on-site video venues in 2004—it now has seven, plus one off-site so far; and in 2005, Fellowship Church in Grapevine, Texas, opened satellite campuses in nearby Plano, Uptown, Dallas, and Alliance.

Indeed, a high percentage of the nation's largest churches and fastest-growing churches are now multi-sites.[2] At each, the motive is to reach more people for Christ by taking the church to where the people are.

But as noted earlier, megachurches have no monopoly on multi-site models. Churches of all sizes have experimented with "niche" ministry approaches as a way of reaching out to people who might not be willing or able to come to the church's original campus. Consider these situations that could perhaps prove durable only through a multi-site framework:

> Megachurches have no monopoly on multi-site models.

Prison Church. Lake Pointe Church in Rockwall, Texas, brings two weekly services to a local correctional facility—one for women and one for men.

Cowboy Church. Lake Pointe Church also sponsors a church service, based on a cattle ranch, where everything from clothing to music to speaking style appeals to a cowboy crowd.

Recovery Center Church. North Coast Church in Vista, California, brings a weekly church service to a local residential drug-rehabilitation center.

Beach Church. Gulf Breeze United Methodist Church in Gulf Breeze, Florida, offers "worship at the water" in a restaurant during the summer months.

Nature Church. Christ the King Community Church in Mount Vernon, Washington, offers a "GPS worship service" during the summer. The advertisement says, "You can worship with us if you can find us!" It then offers global positioning system coordinates (and MapQuest as an Internet-search alternative). The designated location is an oceanside, mountaintop, or forest. The idea is to blend people's love of nature with taking the gospel to new altitudes (literally).

Nursing Home Church. First United Methodist Church in Van Alstyne, Texas, has been sponsoring a nursing home service weekly for the last fifteen years, sending a team to a nearby retirement facility.

What's So New?

How are today's multi-site models different from the kind of outreach that churches have traditionally done when trying to demonstrate that lost people matter to God? Four primary ways:

1. *Relationship versus rescue.* The attitude motivating most multi-sites is relational. The desire is to do more than proclaim the gospel, establishing a presence and relationship as well. Even when they're trying to meet the needs of the poor, oppressed, and forgotten, multi-sites are not content to go back home at the end of the day.

2. *Stepping-stone versus limited-service mission.* A multi-site approach becomes a stepping-stone for greater church involvement. When people are released from prison or a residential drug-rehabilitation center, it's natural for them to become involved in the church that they've come to know. When firefighters have Sunday off, it's a short step for them to join people they know at one of the full-service campuses of their fire-station church.

3. *Personalization versus cookie cutter.* Most multi-site locations designate someone as the campus pastor—a face with the place—who personalizes the church. This person, usually surrounded by a team, helps adapt the church service to the unique local context.

4. *Lay empowerment versus clergy dependency.* Multi-site niche churches are not just about touching new people but also about growing a church's ministry capacity—deploying more volunteers. Multi-sites are not another task for the church staff's to-do list as much as a means for more of the church's people to be involved in spreading the gospel in their surrounding community and affinity groups.

How Well Do *You* Hear Opportunity Knocking?

Conventional church wisdom says, "Once we fill our sanctuary, then we raise the money and build it bigger. That's what other churches do. It's worked for us in the past, and it will no doubt work for us if we need it again."

Multi-site churches have far more options. They show an incredible level of variety in the locations they go to and the type of facilities they select—and the type of people they reach as a result. Each variation opens up new opportunities for those who have eyes to see.

Has your church gone on autopilot, content with the way things are now? Are there ways you are posting the equivalent of a No Vacancy sign? Have you decided that your best job is to take care of the sheep God has given you, and not leave the ninety-nine to go looking for the one lost sheep? Don't overlook Jesus' compassion-motivated conclusion to that story: "In the same way your Father in heaven is not willing that any of these little ones should be lost" (Matt. 18:14).

Sometimes room for expansion simply doesn't exist, as many urban churches know well. Sometimes you do want to expand, but you have an antagonistic local municipality telling you, "We're not going to let you expand your facilities any further." But are there still people within your church's influence who don't yet have a vital, life-transforming relationship with Jesus Christ?

Maybe you need to lead your church (or church group) in a time of seeking God, asking for eyes to see and ears to hear about the opportunities ahead of you. Remember the story of how God was trying to speak to young Samuel. Samuel heard God but mistook it for his spiritual leader, Eli. The old man wisely advised Samuel, "Go and lie down, and if he calls you, say, 'Speak, LORD, for your servant is listening'" (1 Sam. 3:9). So Samuel kept listening and indeed heard from God.

Too often we want to jump in and give people "the" answer. Too often we want to conclude, "There are no more options because I can't envision any."

But sometimes (more often than not!) God is up to something. And if God wants to entrust more souls into your church's care, he will provide the facilities needed — whether on campus or off.

• •

Workout Where is opportunity knocking for your church? Where could you be reaching out to more people? To get the creative juices flowing, turn to the Opportunity Tournament located below.

Once you've settled on the right opportunity for your church, it's time to sell the dream. In chapter 6, we'll look at how other churches have been able to successfully share the multi-site vision with their congregations.

Below are a number of possible multi-site opportunities, listed in groups of two. For each pair, decide which opportunity is most available, most practical, and has the most potential for outreach for your church. Write the winning opportunity on the line to the right of the pair and continue playing opportunities against each other until you narrow the list down to the most intriguing opportunity for your church. To foster discussion, play the Opportunity Tournament with a group of key leaders, weighing the pros and cons of each opportunity as you go.

Opportunity Tournament

- Available on-site space
- Fire station
- Nursing home
- Recovery center
- Prison
- Theater
- School
- YMCA
- Declining church
- Retail space
- Nursing home
- Restaurant/Club/Dinner theater
- Under-evangelized subgroup
- *Membership cluster
- Empty building
- Other (your unique opportunity)

*This refers to a large group of people from the same area who drive twenty or more minutes each weekend to attend church.

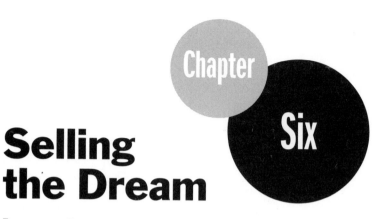

Selling the Dream

Learn how to use effective vision casting, helpful language, and strategic field trips

> If people can't see what God is doing, they stumble all over themselves. — Proverbs 29:18 MESSAGE

Until January 2003, I (Greg) was on the outside, looking in on the multi-site church movement. My colleagues at Leadership Network had put their ears to the ground for the previous two years, listening to the stories of multi-site churches small and large; urban, suburban, and rural; mainline, Bible, and nondenominational; and north, south, east, and west. They consistently noted the impact that the multi-site approach was having in helping churches extend their reach.

When Leadership Network made a decision to establish a new peer-learning leadership community for multi-site churches, I begrudgingly accepted the request to lead it. To be honest, I was a bit skeptical of what I thought to be a "one-model video gig" that was happening in churches. But I scheduled a trip to Chicago and dove in.

During those three days in January 2003, my skepticism turned to awareness and then from awareness to passion for what God was doing. Key to my transformation was the opportunity to experience the vision of Mark Jobe, pastor of New Life Community Church in downtown Chicago. God's vision for New Life first took root in 1997 after its participation in a forty-day national call to prayer and fasting sounded by Bill Bright, the late founder of Campus Crusade for Christ. Mark extended his team's participation, and during those "extra days" of personal spiritual retreat, Mark sensed God's call to lead the church, then averaging 500 in attendance, to reach 1 percent of Chicago's population for Christ. Mark recalls thinking the vision was big but "doable" until he went back to his office and did the actual math. One percent of some three million people translated to 30,000-plus people to be reached!

Mark gathered his team and told them of the call he felt that God had placed on New Life. One team member's immediate response was, "Well, we certainly can't build a building big enough for the vision, so God must have something in mind that involves multiple locations."

Thus the New Life Community Church multi-site vision was born. To draw an analogy from history, during World War II some 300,000 British troops were pinned by Hitler at Dunkirk with their backs to the sea. The only way out was to retreat across the water. But how do you move 300,000 people by water? There isn't a boat big enough to carry them. The call went out to anyone with a boat to rescue them. One thousand boats arrived, and over the course of ten days, all of the troops were evacuated. They couldn't build a boat big enough to move 300,000 people, but 1,000 little boats could do the job. Likewise, for Mark Jobe, no single church can impact all of Chicago, but a church in 1,000 different locations could.

Mark's vision now finds its growing expression in eight campuses serving some 2,600 people across racial, ethnic, cultural, and socioeconomic lines. "Wealthier" campuses are investing in smaller, "poorer" campuses, not out of a sense of philanthropy but because they are members of the same body of Christ called New Life Community Church, Chicago. The exchange goes both ways because smaller campuses with fewer financial resources often demonstrate depth in community involvement, showing other campuses how to develop significant relational equity in the community.

At the conference, I also learned that my stereotype of a "one-model video gig" was completely naive. Most New Life locations have their own campus pastor who does the preaching. Each site embodies the DNA of the New Life movement, yet each has tailored its ministry locally.

Actually, I shouldn't have been surprised. The story of New Life Chicago is simply a microcosm of the body of Christ being lived out throughout the city of Chicago. The same impulse is behind multi-site churches in cities and towns around the world.

Perhaps you've caught a vision for multi-site ministry and are wondering, "Now what?" Perhaps as you have begun to cast the vision, you have bumped into a skeptical elder, lay leader, or staff member—as I was before my trip to Chicago. What follows are some initial steps people took as they explored whether God was calling them to extend their ministry through additional campuses and then as they built goal ownership among their church.

Tell the Story and Give Ownership

Mark Jobe's story is instructive about what is involved in selling the multi-site dream. Mark listened to God, gathered his leaders, and presented what he sensed God was calling New Life to do: develop a church that would reach 1 percent of Chicago (30,000 people). He then asked his team for ideas about how they might accomplish this task. Mark told the story and invited his team to help him birth the model that would move New Life toward their God-given vision. Mark understood that people will support a world they help create.

> Mark understood that people will support a world they help create.

Mark repeated this process many times. Selling the dream is a recurring task for leaders in all contexts, but especially in multi-site churches. Mark and other directional leaders continue to tell the story and invite others to be part of a multi-site church. They do so through preaching, church websites, New Life communication pieces, and occasional all-church meetings that gather some 2,600 people from eight campuses in one place to celebrate what God is doing.

Give Your Team a Firsthand Taste

Nothing helps people get inside a new idea like test-driving it for themselves! One of the best ways to develop a story is to give your leaders and congregation an opportunity to experience a multi-site church so that they're part of the story. Depending on your location and budget, this can be accomplished in a variety of ways. Options include:

1. *Ask around locally.* Many churches in the prayer and investigation stage of becoming a multi-site congregation do on-site visits with local multi-site churches. The idea is to experience it firsthand and to observe what pieces seem to work best—an experiential "best practices" approach.

2. *Travel to a model.* Many leadership teams get on an airplane to attend a conference hosted by a multi-site church or simply to visit a high-visibility multi-site church. For example, you're learning much about Seacoast Church because lead author Geoff Surratt has used many Seacoast illustrations in this book. Seacoast offers "Hands On" experiences several times a year. Learn more at www.seacoast.org.

   Whenever possible, try to visit at least two different sites, because then you'll be less likely to clone what you see and more likely to contextualize it to fit your situation. "The way church A presents itself is a good model for us, but the way church B has built its team will fit us better, and the financial model at church C is the best parallel for how we structure our budget." (See appendix C for a list of the multi-site churches cited in this book, plus an Internet link to multi-site churches across North America.)

3. *Visit vicariously online.* Many church leadership teams also do "virtual" visits to multi-campus churches by browsing their websites. For a list of churches presented in this book and their websites see appendix C.

4. *Read.* Besides reading and discussing this book, go to Leadership Network's online library for various multi-site reports (www.leadnet.org/LC_Resources.asp?LC=MultiSiteChurches). Consider also subscribing to *Leadership Network Advance,* a free e-publication, for periodic updates on multi-site and other innovative approaches to doing church in the twenty-first century (www.leadnet.org/epubs_signup.asp). Only a handful of books currently exist that discuss the multi-site movement; most of the ones in print are listed in the endnotes.

5. *Experiment.* Ask your staff to develop an experimental worship service to be held in your multi-purpose room, a nearby school, etc. Gauge the response, and if it seems to work, prayerfully go for it.

Choose Appropriate Selling Points

The church's senior-level leaders, staff and lay leaders alike, must lead the charge in championing the vision. As Lyle Schaller emphasizes, the often-overlooked first step is to create dissatisfaction with the status quo.[1] As people become aware that the present reality is inadequate, they will want and should receive an understanding of the *why*. Effective vision casting clearly articulates the advantages of employing a multi-site strategy in ministry. Among the benefits are the ways multi-site:

> The often-overlooked first step is to create dissatisfaction with the status quo.

1. Brings together the best aspects of larger churches and smaller churches
2. Increases the total number of available seats during optimal worship times
3. Overcomes geographic barriers when a church facility is landlocked or tightly zoned
4. Enables untapped talent to emerge each time a new venue or site is opened
5. Mobilizes volunteers through an added variety of ministry opportunities
6. Increases options of location and sometimes of worship style too
7. Assists in reaching friends and family unwilling to travel a great distance to church
8. Accelerates the climate for diversity, creativity, and innovation in ministry
9. Improves a church's stewardship of funds and resources
10. Enables a church to extend itself into niches like a cancer ward or an office complex
11. Helps a congregation see evidences of how it's part of a larger kingdom mission

12. Models and trains people for church planting elsewhere
13. Provides a pipeline for the development of emerging leaders and future staff

Cite Prophets as Appropriate

As you cast the vision, it is sometimes helpful to share what noted leaders are saying about the multi-site movement. Sometimes it's as simple as referencing a magazine article, such as this editorial comment in *Leadership*, a journal for pastors: "The multi-site church is a phenomenon that you will no doubt be hearing about in the future."[2]

Bill Easum, principal church consultant for Easum, Bandy, and Associates (www.easumbandy.com) and author of several books, including *Beyond the Box: Innovative Churches That Work*, says it more strongly: "The multi-site movement will explode over the next few decades." Why? "It is how the church grew in the early centuries and it is how the church is exploding in other parts of the world in cell and house churches. Churches with limited land and a Great Commission mindset will find multi-site the most economic way to be faithful and grow."[3]

> "Churches with limited land and a Great Commission mindset will find multi-site the most economic way to be faithful and grow."
> – Bill Easum and Dave Travis, *Beyond the Box*

Bill is convinced the movement has great significance for the future. "I get as excited about this movement as I do the church planting movements underway," he says. "It is not just another program *du jour*. It is a way of life; a way of responding to God's call to be the church."

Charles Arn affirms, "The satellite church is just the next — and not likely the last — step that builds on the way Jesus went from town to town, and sent his disciples to do the same, in order to introduce the gospel to as many as possible. Perhaps it's time for more churches to take a look around at what God is blessing and simply do more of it."

Avoid Language Traps

We all know the age-old adage "A picture paints a thousand words." This can have both positive and negative implications. In presenting your multi-site story, avoiding certain "word-picture land mines" will accelerate your church's acceptance of the vision.

Almost every multi-site church decides not to refer to the original location as the "main campus" or the "mother church" or even the "mother ship." This terminology can easily communicate to the venues and sites birthed from the original campus that they are second-class. Not only can this negatively impact the motivation of new campuses and their leadership; it can also create harmful feelings on the original campus if the new locations begin to be seen as a drain on the work being done at the "real campus" or "more important main site."

Some of the multi-site pioneers addressed these language-trap challenges by naming the new venues and locations geographically or according to worship style. For example, at Seacoast, we (Geoff) refer internally to each campus by its geographical location (Long Point Road, West Ashley, Irmo, etc.). Externally, all of our campuses are simply called Seacoast. In contrast, North Coast Church in Vista, California, identifies its on-site venues by worship style — Traditions, The Edge, Video Café, and most recently Country Gospel. North Coast's original worship site is presented as just one of the many names, in this case, North Coast Live.

In addition to renaming campuses, some churches have developed job descriptions that communicate their commitment to the broader multi-site vision. Bruxy Cavey, senior pastor at The Meeting House, says that he and the other senior leaders are not the staff of the main (original) campus but rather the staff of the vision. In a similar manner, their board members (elders) are overseers of the vision at the now five campuses.

Listen Well to Trustworthy Critics — and Pray for Discernment

The book *Culture Shift* is cowritten by two seasoned pastors, Robert Lewis and Wayne Cordeiro (who both serve multi-site churches, by the way).[4] It coaches church leaders on how to identify the present "corporate culture" of their congregation. Then it guides readers on how to shift their church's culture to align better with the kingdom values of their church's stated mission. It advocates the use of focus groups, surveys, and other tools for good listening.

Noting that every church has one (or more) chronic grumps, coauthor Robert Lewis discusses how to sort through various criticisms that arise.

> Do we listen to everyone's feedback? Yes and no. It's easy to identify feedback comments that come from the kind of person Gordon MacDonald calls a VDP—a very draining person. That's someone who always has an axe to grind, and who feels we're never good enough. Those comments are rarely constructive or helpful.
>
> Instead, I want to hear from healthy people—the growing ones. There are certain people in our church who I know, "If they're happy, the whole church is happy." They represent the kind of people we'd never want to lose: those whose lives are growing and bearing fruit, who do the most effective ministry, and who make the greatest impact long-term. By listening to them, our church can gain rich insights into how God is moving and what ministry items are working best.[5]

As you introduce multi-site ideas, you can expect a degree of opposition. Pray hard, asking God for discernment, asking if the criticisms reveal a blind spot in your planning.

Whenever possible, pray with your critics. An important step toward building trust is to pray together. God delights in bringing unity to his church. Distrust often melts away when people pray together with open, sincere hearts.

Link to History and Scripture

In some ways, the multi-site approach is not new. Some argue that the church of the New Testament era was multi-site in many cities. A case can be made that as church history unfolded, the church had many multi-site expressions, from mission stations to Methodist circuit riders to branch Sunday schools done by bus ministry. Digital technologies, combined with growing social acceptance of branch-church ideas, have made a new movement possible today. Craig Groeschel, pastor of Life Church in Oklahoma City, has Methodist roots. He likes to comment that the move from horseback preacher to satellite broadcast is simply a shift from circuit rider to closed-circuit rider!

We're at that same kind of point in history again: as we put the gospel into the normal communication path of our current culture, there will be a fruitful response because people—from seekers to disciples—receive it in a form they can comprehend.

In short, the Word of God doesn't have to be read live to be active! The Word, energized by the Holy Spirit, can be printed or spoken, recorded on a CD, downloaded on an Ipod, or transmitted by satellite. Because it is God's Word, it—like God—transcends time. "For you have been born again, not of perishable seed, but of imperishable, through the living and enduring word of God" (1 Peter 1:23).

You might say that the idea of "one church, many locations" began with the persecution of the first Christ-followers in Jerusalem. When Stephen was put to death and the believers scattered, a new congregation was formed in Antioch. The Antioch group was not seen as a separate body but as an extension of the Jerusalem church and functioned under the authority of Peter and the apostles in Jerusalem. Barnabas effectively became the first campus pastor when he was sent to Antioch to care for the new congregation. As the good news spread throughout Asia and into Europe, new congregations were formed, but they were all connected back to the church at Jerusalem as evidenced by the council that was held in Acts 15.

It was not uncommon for these congregations to all experience the same teaching when they met together. Paul wrote to the church at Colosse, "After this letter has been read to you, see that it is also read in the church of the Laodiceans and that you in turn read the letter from Laodicea" (Col. 4:16). Paul used letters to communicate with the various churches because they were the best tools available in his time. It's not hard to imagine Paul using DVDs, videoconferences, and satellite feeds to spread the gospel if he were in twenty-first century North America.

> It's not hard to imagine Paul using DVDs, videoconferences, and satellite feeds to spread the gospel if he were in twenty-first century North America.

The Word Doesn't Have to Be Live to Be Active

On a recent Sunday at Seacoast Summerville, a videocast campus, one of the many new faces that morning was Shelly (not her real name), who was passing through town on her way to Florida. She had left her husband of eighteen years behind in Virginia, unsure if she'd ever return. She had lived in Summerville as a little girl and, on the spur of the moment, decided to spend a couple of days there as she tried to sort out her future. She found Seacoast in the yellow pages and decided to attend; it sounded like her church back home. The video message that weekend was called "For Better or Worse" on rebuilding a broken marriage. Shelly knew it was no accident that she was in that church on that weekend. With tears in her eyes, she decided to return to Virginia to give her marriage one more try. A few days later, Shelly called to say that she and her husband had decided to try to work things out; could she get a copy of the message video she had heard the weekend before? The writer of Hebrews says: "The Word of God is living and active. Sharper than any double-edged sword, it penetrates even to dividing soul and spirit, joints and marrow; it judges the thoughts and attitudes of the heart" (Heb. 4:12).

The power of the Word isn't limited by the medium.

The power of the Word isn't limited by the medium.

Keep Focus on the Fruit

When we first proposed the idea of doing off-site campuses at Seacoast, I (Geoff) had a line of people at my office door, telling me why it wouldn't work. Why do we want to replicate ministries that we do poorly at the original campus? We don't have enough leaders, volunteers, and musicians for the services we are already doing, how can we do more? Budgets are stretched tight, how can we spend money on additional campuses? I wanted to argue with them, to show them that we had a divine mandate from God, but they were right. Some of our ministries were held together with rubber bands and duct tape, we had no backups for our music teams, and our finances were so tight we had to bring WD-40 to budget meetings. Going multi-site didn't make sense, except for the fact that we had no other choice.

To help the naysayers catch the vision, we positioned our first off-site campus as an experiment. "Multi-site is working in San Diego, Chicago, and Atlanta," I'd respond to the line of critics, "so let's see if it could work in South Carolina." After that first experiment was successful, the line at my door got a little shorter; after we opened our second, third, and fourth campuses, the membership in the Seacoast Order of Multi-Site Critics had shrunk considerably. Nine campuses and 3,000 new attendees later, we're down to one gripey old man who also thinks indoor plumbing is a bad idea.

Our approach at Seacoast to selling the multi-site vision now is similar to Jesus' response when John the Baptist sent his disciples to ask Jesus if he was the real deal. John had been thrown in prison and was waiting to have his head handed to him on a platter; now he was having second thoughts about his mission. Jesus didn't rebuke John or his disciples. He simply told them, "Go back and report to John what you hear and see: The blind receive sight, the lame walk, those who have leprosy are cured, the deaf hear, the dead are raised, and the good news is preached to the poor" (Matt. 11:4 – 5).

●●

Workout

One day as Seacoast's pastor, Greg Surratt (Geoff's older brother), was discussing our multi-site experiment with a key lay leader in the church, Greg said, "If this thing works …" Before he could finish his sentence, the layman interrupted and said, "The jury is in, pal. Multi-site works. Case closed." Greg realized that the man was right: the experiment was over. It was at that point that Seacoast truly became "one church, many campuses." Our primary vision caster was now fully on board.

In the pages that follow we have provided a workout for the primary vision caster of your church to use as a personal vision check. Once the vision is twenty-twenty, it's time to hit the pocketbook. Join us in chapter 7, where we'll figure out how to pay for all these new campuses.

For this workout, you will need a notebook; a beach, mountain, lake, or other place of tranquility and inspiration; and time to be alone with God and your dreams. Ask God to remove the scales from your eyes so that you can see what he sees when he looks at the future of your church. Use at least one full notebook page to answer each question.

1. If nothing were impossible and God were to bless your church beyond all that you could ask or imagine, what would multi-site look like at your church in three years? How many campuses would you have? How many people would you be reaching? How would your church have changed?

Create a present-tense word picture of your new church. Describe the campuses, the leaders, and the lives that have been changed.

2. Why do you feel led toward this vision? What is attractive about leading a multi-site church?

3. What do you need to learn before you can lead your church toward this new vision?

4. What do you need to see before you embark on this journey? Where do you need to visit?

5. Who do you need to inspire to take this multi-site journey with you? How will you inspire them?

6. What obstacles must be overcome before you can begin the journey?

7. What is your next step?

Who's Going to Pay for This?

Discover how to do multi-site in ways your church can afford

> Suppose one of you wants to build a tower. Will he not first sit down and estimate the cost to see if he has enough money to complete it?
> — LUKE 14:28

Nappanee Missionary Church, located in north-central Indiana's Amish country, is a rural congregation. Nappanee's population is just over 6,000 and is truly heartland America, with two drugstores, one theater, and a nine-person police force. The church, founded in the late 1800s, has grown to a weekly worship attendance of some 2,700 adults and children under the leadership of Dave Engbrecht, who has served there since 1979.

How has the church accommodated the growth? In addition to three Sunday morning services in the sanctuary, the church sponsors a video venue in its gym, known as Connection. Characterized as "next-generation worship," a live band plays contemporary music, and then the pastor's message is played on a big projection screen. It's a casual environment with a coffeehouse feel, both theater-style and table seating, and regular use of drama and other creative forms of communication. The student ministries pastor serves as the campus pastor. Typical attendance in the gym is 400. Connection uses a DVD recording of the sermon from the first service (8:15 a.m.) when it meets at 10:45 a.m.

Nappanee's second video venue, New Life Fellowship, opened in January 2005. Located thirty miles away in the even more rural area of Topeka/Shipshewana, it meets in a grade school cafeteria and averaged 190 children and adults during its first six months. Scott Engbrecht (the senior pastor's son) is the campus pastor. New Life Fellowship uses a DVD recording of the previous week's teaching and has live worship. "We believe these venues, done correctly, will enable us to keep expanding the ministry," says Dave.

Counting the Costs

Multi-site ministry expansion like Nappanee's sounds great, but who's going to pay for it? At most churches, from new start-ups to rapidly expanding megachurches, every penny of the annual budget is spoken for. From adding staff to upgrading equipment to repairing what the church already has, a pool of money is seldom available for funding an adventure as aggressive as starting another campus five, ten, or one hundred miles away.

If your church is in prayerful discussion about joining the world of multiple-location churches, it is important to count the costs.

To compound the problem, underfunding is one of the main reasons for the failure of any new venture, whether it's a new business, a new church, or a new campus. If your church is in prayerful discussion about joining the world of multiple-location churches, it is important to count the costs.

The first cost to count is the price of not opening a second campus. Churches that are not growing and do *not* have a mission to expand beyond their own neighborhoods will incur no extra financial costs; they can continue doing church just as they always have. In many cases, however, they are still paying a cost: the cost of not gaining ground in obedience to Jesus' command to make disciples.

For churches that are growing or that want to be more missional, however, the costs of not becoming multi-site can be quite high. Some of the options for growing churches include:

1. *Adding services.* This is a relatively low-cost solution to managing growth. Most churches have found, however, that only a limited number of services can be added without burning out their lead teachers and staff. The law of diminishing returns also comes into play since the new services are added away from the Sunday morning "prime time" for new attendees. Churches experiencing rapid growth often run out of practical new service times and energy at about the same time.

2. *Building a larger building.* This is the traditional answer to growth, but building can be very expensive. As we will explore later in this chapter, opening an off-site campus is almost always much less expensive than building a bigger building.

3. *Doing nothing.* This strategy almost always curbs the growth, but the cost in lost opportunity is very high.

Once the decision to go multi-site is made, the next question is, "Just how much is this thing going to cost anyway?" (This is often the first question of the same deacon or staff member who doesn't understand why the children's ministry needs a video projector. "They didn't even have filmstrip projectors when I was in Sunday school, and I turned out fine.")

The answer is entirely dependent on the model that resonates best with the overall mission of the church. For those who adopt the low-risk model, starting a new campus can be as inexpensive as starting a new small group. Seacoast Church invests $75,000 in its new campus plants, which covers the cost of all equipment and marketing as well as a few months of the campus pastor's salary. Churches who use the regional-campus model, however, will usually invest several hundred thousand to over a million dollars in duplicating the experience of their primary location. Much of the investment is in lighting, sound, and video equipment and in securing large facilities to get the new campus off to a fast start. Except for very large megachurches, most churches opening their first off-site campus will invest between $50,000 and $150,000.

Build for the Grandkids No More

For many years, when you talked to church leaders about new buildings, you often heard, "We want to leave a legacy. We want to build something that will be around for our grandchildren." In recent days, especially in the multi-site world, church leaders have realized that this legacy may be more a hindrance to ministry than the gift it was intended to be. Large, expensive, specialized church facilities leave their heirs with high operating costs, big maintenance bills, and buildings that may or may not coincide with the future needs of the ministry.

Today's conversations about facilities are punctuated with commitments to flexibility in both design and financing arrangements. Many churches are converting existing space that has served as a warehouse, "big box" retail space, or even faltering churches. Whether a purchase or a lease arrangement, the costs of rehabilitating existing facilities often prove to be smaller, representing greater stewardship as resources once devoted to building a bigger building can be reallocated to starting new campuses or other ministry initiatives.

Are the days of building new facilities completely over? Hardly. But as the multi-site movement grows, building a new building does not always equal building a bigger worship space. In Vista, California, North Coast Church, which draws over 6,000 people in weekend worship services, is in the process of building a new facility that will accommodate its video-venue model by having multiple worship spaces, of which the largest seating capacity will be only about 1,500.[1]

Another essential part of the facility conversation involves shared facilities. Throughout the pages of this book, you will find stories of churches that are sharing facilities with businesses, schools, community centers, nonprofit organizations, and other churches. These relationships create space at a fraction of the cost associated with building a new facility.[2]

● ● ●

Funding Multiple Sites

"Great," the penny-pinching deacon interjects, "but what if this really goes well and we want to start another site, where will that money come from? Multi-site churches have found a variety of answers to this important question:

> *Special offerings.* When the leaders at Life Church felt God calling them to open a fifth campus in Oklahoma City, they went to the people. The first idea had been to follow a traditional fundraising route, asking people to give money to fund bricks or chairs in the new site. But they felt that might limit people's vision for the new project. Pastor Craig Groeschel decided to simply take the vision to the people and see what would happen. One weekend, with very little fanfare or preparation, he clearly shared what he felt God had called them to do and then asked the people to give. In one weekend, the people gave over $1 million toward a campus they would never attend. Life Church opened its South Campus in spring 2005 and is now reaching over 2,000 additional people at this new site.
>
> In 2004, Seacoast faced a major dilemma: after years of negotiation, we were finally given permission from the city to expand our facilities at our original location. How would a capital stewardship campaign play out at our off-site campuses? How could we continue to fund new campuses while pouring millions of dollars into a new building? How could we ask people to give toward a children's building one hundred miles away while their own children were crawling through gummy bears at the theater where their campus met?
>
> *10 – 10 – 80.* To answer these questions, we (Geoff) created what we called a 10 – 10 – 80 capital campaign. The first 10 percent of what people gave would go toward missions projects, the next 10 percent would fund new campus start-ups, and the remaining 80 percent would fund a capital improvement project at the individual campuses. In this way, we were able to continue opening new campuses, and only the people at the original campus gave toward the new building there. People responded by pledging to give $15 million over three years toward the

various projects, allowing us to build the needed building, fund missions projects around the world, and continue to open new campuses.

Pay it forward. From the beginning of the multi-site adventure at Christ the King in Washington, Pastor Dave Browning has had a vision to continuously open new campuses as opportunities arise. To fund this vision, they have developed what they call the "Pay It Forward" plan. From the beginning, each new campus pays 10 percent of their budget into the Pay It Forward fund. This fund is in turn used to cover the small initial investment of 10 percent in starting new campuses. In this way, the more campuses Christ the King opens, the more campuses they can open in the future.

Pay it locally. Sometimes a campus can be virtually self-sustaining from day one, especially if done as a low-risk approach. For example, Dave Browning reports, "When our Samish Island Worship Center opened in 2003, nearly all the costs were absorbed by the volunteers involved. They rented the community center. They purchased sound and video equipment. They publicized the opening."

Tapping into grants. Healing Place Church, Baton Rouge, Louisiana (introduced in chapter 4), has secured more than $6 million in government grants to address needs from their faith-based perspective. "We're very involved in caring for hurting people," says Pastor Dino Rizzo, "whether it is AIDS orphans in Africa or those living in one of the nation's lowest-income communities in nearby Donaldsonville." The Garden in Indianapolis (introduced in chapter 4), cultivates an even broader range of grants, ranging from grants from family-based foundations to a grant from its denomination, the local conference of the United Methodist Church.

Other options. In addition to Life Church's special offering, Seacoast's 10-10-80 capital campaign, and Christ the King's Pay It Forward fund, churches have used a variety of models to fund new campuses. Some, such as Willow Creek, have made multi-site part of a capital campaign designed primarily to raise funds for expanding current facilities. Willow Creek seeded their regional strategy as a part of its Chapter Two capital campaign. Other churches have started their new sites from their operating budgets, much as they would begin new ministries. Some churches use part of their designated missions money to start new outreaches into a new community. Occasionally leaders in a community will raise the money themselves, or the core team will be challenged to commit to give toward the new campus, much as they would pledge to a capital campaign.

Early in the multi-site process, a church will need to find a sustainable financial model for replication.

Day-to-Day Funding

Intrigued by the relatively low cost of start-up and convinced that there are ways to raise the seed money, the filmstrip-deprived deacon now wants to know, "What about operating costs? Once we get this thing off the ground, how are we going to keep it flying?" First, the expense of operating a second, third, and fourth campus is often much less than operating the original site. In highlighting the advantages of smaller off-site campuses, Dave Browning notes, "To serve coffee for thousands, you need a $10,000 commercial brewer. To serve coffee for a hundred, you need two fifty-cup brewers that you can buy anywhere for $50." When an off-site campus is located in a rented facility, several costs are reduced. Maintenance costs are low, utilities are often included in the lease, and facility personnel seldom need to be hired. In their book, *The Nomadic Church*, Bill Easum and Pete Theodore say this about the advantages of rented facilities: "The capital needed to acquire land and then design, build, and maintain a permanent facility is astronomical. The closer you are to a population center, the higher the costs. And because land is a limited resource, its expense will only increase. Financial bondage is not uncommon for stationary churches."[3]

The expense of operating a second, third, and fourth campus is often much less than operating the original site.

The real savings, however, are in the synergy of shared resources. Two, three, or four campuses often share the same bookkeeper, the

Quick Facts: Funding the Multi-Site Vision

An Overview of Five Different Types of Multi-Site Locations

Church name	Christ Fellowship	First Baptist Church Windermere	LifeChurch.tv	National Community Church	North Coast Church
Site name	The Ascent at Christ Fellowship CityPlace	First Baptist Church Windermere at Lake Buena Vista	LifeChurch.tv Tulsa	National Community Church at Ebenezers	North Coast @ Madison
Site description	Performing arts center in heart of downtown shopping, restaurant, office, and condo district (shared-use facility)	Existing church building	Warehouse (repurposed existing space)	Church-run coffee shop (unique venue)	Public middle school
Site number	Third	Second	Third	Third	Third
How facility was obtained	Rent (Sunday mornings only)	Donation through merger	Purchase (converted space)	Purchase (built it)	Rent (Sunday mornings only)
Funding sources (including borrowed moneys)	Overall church budget (didn't take special offering)	Overall church budget (included special offering)	Overall church budget (didn't take special offering)	Tithes from church members, revenues from coffee shop, loan (mortgage)	Overall church budget (didn't take special offering)

Church name	Christ Fellowship	First Baptist Church Windermere	LifeChurch.tv	National Community Church	North Coast Church
Expect site to become self-supporting?	Yes, by 1 year	Yes, by 1 year	Yes, by 2 years	No	Yes, by 1 year
Payback expectation?	None	None	None	None	None
Start-up cost for site (not including staff)	$75,000	$50,000 (facility renovation and landscaping)	$110,000 for 2000 launch; $1.3 million in 2002 for major expansion	$60,000 (entire building is $2,000,000)	$85,000 (two trucks to store and transport equipment)
Percentage of overall church budget represented by this site (including staff)	Less than 5%	10%	9%	10% (projected)	2%
Site attendance 12 months after launch	2,000 (projected)	125	400 (12 months after initial launch in 2002); 1,200 (6 months after relaunch in 2004)	150 (projected)	275
Location of original campus	Palm Beach Gardens, FL	Windermere, FL	Oklahoma City, OK	Washington D.C.	Vista, CA

Denomination	Nondenominational	Southern Baptist	Evangelical Covenant	Assemblies of God	Evangelical Free Church
Church age	20 years	38 years	9 years	8 years	27 years
Year church became multi-site	2004	2000	2001	2004	1998
Internet address	www.gochristfellowship.com	www.fbcwindermere.com	www.lifechurch.tv	www.theaterchurch.com	www.northcoastchurch.com
Similar examples	Stillwater United Methodist Church, Dayton, OH (www.stillwaterumc.org), partnered with an area YMCA to develop a campus in 2002, which has worked very well. The partnership continues to grow into multiple ministries (preschool, fitness, teen ministries, and shared facilities).	RockPointe Alliance Church, Calgary, AB (www.bvalliance.ca), merged with another congregation in 2004. After some difficult transition months, both campuses are growing, with 5 services between them.	North Point Community Church, Atlanta, GA (www.northpoint.org), refurbished a Harris Teeter grocery store as its second site. Lake Pointe Baptist Church, Rockwall, TX (www.lakepointe.org) bought an old Oshman's department store for an additional site. New Life Chicago (www.newlifechicago.com) converted a light-manufacturing facility.	St. Luke's United Methodist Church, Indianapolis, IN (www.the-garden.org), has 2 satellite congregations; 1 in a dinner theater, and 1 in a catering facility.	Northland – A Church Distributed (www.northlandcc.org) uses Lyman High School for one of its locations. Fellowship Church, Grapevine, TX (www.FellowshipChurch.org), leases space at North Dallas High School for one of its sites. Christ the King Church (www.ctkonline.com), uses public schools for 5 of its 15 locations.

same videographer, and the same small groups pastor. All the bills can be paid from one business office; there is one insurance plan and one payroll system. Because of the reduced cost of operating additional sites, many multi-site churches have found that their off-site locations are often self-sustaining within a few months.

Part of the answer to our deacon friend's question about day-to-day funding depends on the multi-site model chosen. Others have asked, "Whose purse is it?" There are a variety of ways to handle money at off-site campuses. For some churches, such as Seacoast, each campus is considered a separate entity in a sort of franchise model. While there is one master budget and one bank account, each campus has a separate budget and pays part of its income to the central budget to cover operating costs and to help fund new campuses. At Life Church in Oklahoma City, all the income is put into one master budget. Each campus has its own operating budget, like ministries in a traditional church, but the campus budget is not based solely on the income at that campus. A third approach is the "fee for service" model. In this case, the campus is completely separate financially from the sponsoring campus. Anything the sponsoring campus provides is offered for a fee to the off-site campuses.

> The real savings, however, are in the synergy of shared resources.

• •

Workout

Now it's time to sharpen the number-two pencils and get to work. How much will your first multi-site campus or venue cost? How are you going to pay for it? Budgeting for your first off-site campus is a challenging exercise. It is unknown territory for most churches, and it's difficult to find benchmarks from other churches that are applicable in your situation.

This workout will help you answer these crucial questions. We have provided a budget worksheet to help focus your thoughts as you begin the budget process. So gather your financial thinkers (the men and women who dream in rows and columns), technical wizards, and detail checkers and get to work on your plan. You will also need to include the senior pastor and key leaders from the ministry areas that will be reproduced at the new site.

1. How would you describe the vision for the new campus?

   a. Trial balloon (low risk, minimum investment)

   b. Controlled experiment (medium risk, intermediate investment)

   c. Bet the farm (high risk, large investment)

2. What term best describes the new campus?

   a. A franchise of the original campus

   b. A company-owned store

   c. A branch office of the church

3. Where will the start-up capital for the new site come from?

   a. General fund

   b. Missions/outreach fund

   c. Special offering(s)

   d. Capital stewardship campaign

   e. Other _____

4. How much are you willing to invest in start-up capital and operating costs for the first year at the new campus?

5. When do you expect the new campus to break even?

   a. Within six months

   b. Within one year

   c. One to two years

   d. Two to three years

   e. Three years or more

   f. The new campus will never break even

6. Who will set the budget for the new campus? _____

7. How will the budget be handled?
    a. As a ministry of the original campus
    b. As a separate entity
    c. As a line item in the general budget
    d. Other _____

8. Who will make decisions on long-term financial obligations at the new campus? (rents, leases, major purchases, capital improvements)

   _____

Sample Start-up Budget

	Cost		Cost
OUTSIDE		**CHILDREN'S AUDITORIUM**	
►Signs		►Sound	
►Parking team equipment		►Video	
►Lobby		►Lighting	
►Bookstore		►Stage	
►Café		►Electrical	
►Information desk		►Props	
►Supplies		►Supplies	
ADULT AUDITORIUM		**NURSERY**	
►Sound		►Registration	
►Video		►Mats	
►Lighting		►Toys	
►Stage		►Furniture	
►Electrical		►Miscellaneous	
►Supplies		►Supplies	
TRANSPORTATION/ STORAGE		**PRESCHOOL**	
►Trailer(s)		►Video	
►Storage unit/container		►Sound	
		►Toys	
		►Furniture	
		►Barriers (to divide children's areas)	
		►Supplies	
		TOTAL	

Sample Operating Budget		
Based On a Template Developed by Seacoast Church		
INCOME	Seacoast	Your church
▶ Attendees	250	
▶ Average annual giving per person	$650	
Total	$162,500	
EXPENSES	Seacoast	Your church
▶ Compensation	$58,500	
▶ Overhead	$29,250	
▶ Ministries	$14,625	
▶ Administration fees (Paid back to Seacoast)	$29,250	
▶ Missions	$14,625	
Total	$146,250	
SAFETY NET	Seacoast	Your church
▶ Income	$162,500	
▶ Expenses	$146,250	
Net income/loss	$ 6,250	

Launching the Mission

Evaluate these common factors in the successful launch of a second location

> While they were worshiping the Lord and fasting, the Holy Spirit said, "Set apart for me Barnabas and Saul for the work to which I have called them." So after they had fasted and prayed, they placed their hands on them and sent them off. — Acts 13:2-3

In 1987, I (Warren) led a small group to start a mission church. We were the first new church in our community in more than one hundred years. Yet dozens of new Jewish yeshivas had been started in the last decade alone, as the local population was rapidly changing from Catholic to Orthodox Jewish and Ultra-Orthodox Jewish residents.

In this climate full of uphill challenges, I did everything wrong. I didn't build a healthy core group, I didn't work from my God-given strengths, I didn't sense the importance of building trust relationships with local officials, I didn't know how to help our small nucleus work their webs of influence, and I didn't have the basic skills of casting a compelling vision and tapping into whatever momentum God was providing for us. I had read everything I could find about church planting. Yet I still needed a lot of help!

Fortunately, if I started over today, I would have plenty of good tools to guide me. For many churches, starting the first off-campus satellite is much like planting a new church. The following material reviews the basics of church planting as it applies to how Seacoast Church launches an additional campus and also emphasizes the many advantages of being an extension of an established church rather than starting solo from scratch.

People Identification

At Seacoast, we (Geoff) have developed a routine for launching new campuses through a scientific process we like to call "trial and error." When we don't know what steps to take we try something—or anything! If it works, we take credit for it and put it in a book (like this one). If it fails, we sweep it under the rug as quickly as possible and pretend it never happened. Each step of our highly refined process either has been carefully tested and has succeeded in the past or it's something we're pretty sure will work when we get around to trying it in the future.

The first step in launching a new campus for Seacoast is to prayerfully find the right leaders. The right leaders are the key to the eventual success or failure of a campus. The most crucial leader for us is the campus pastor. For this role, we look for a high-energy individual who is a recognized leader, a team builder, a developer of other leaders and has a passion for the community he is going into. Every time we find that kind of leader, the new campus succeeds. Our leadership-training model is to help develop the leader along three stages: leading a small group, leading a cluster of groups in a worship café, and ultimately, leading a campus, as illustrated in the diagram below.

Seacoast Launch Strategy

| Person | Group | Café | Campus |

Along with a campus pastor, we want to identify three other key leaders during the prelaunch phase. We look for a worship leader to oversee all the aspects of music at the new campus, a children's ministry director, and a small groups coach. We then ask these leaders to begin identifying and developing their own team leaders well in advance of the campus launch.

While we are identifying and training the key leaders, we are also looking for the right community for a new campus. We ask three crucial questions in deciding where to put our next campus.

1. *Are there people in the area with a connection to Seacoast?* Our first step is to mine our database to find out where people are coming from to attend an existing Seacoast campus. We look for communities that have a high concentration of Seacoast attendees and are more than ten minutes away from an existing campus.

2. *Is there a need in the community for a church like Seacoast?* We try to avoid competition with other growing, like-minded churches in a community. We want to identify communities where unchurched people do not have a Seacoast-type ministry to attend.

3. *Is the community growing?* We prefer to locate our new campuses in growing communities. We find that a flux of new residents in the area can provide a start-up campus with needed leadership and growth without draining other churches in the area.

Once we have targeted a community for a new campus, we begin to narrow down our selection of an exact location within that community. While the first key to a successful campus is the right leadership, a close second is the right location. A poor location can cripple a new campus. We look for a high-visibility site in a growing area surrounded by housing developments.

Ideally, we want a site that has an auditorium that will seat a minimum of 300 adults, a space for at least 60 children that is divided into four areas, and parking for 200 cars. Why those numbers? A momentum kicks in if we can reach a certain critical mass in terms of size.

When we opened our campus in Greenville, South Carolina, we decided to break all these rules, so we launched the campus in a convention center. We had parking for 10,000 cars and potential seating for 50,000 people, but to get to our service, you had to walk 412 miles from where you parked your car and then had to navigate a maze of 123 separate auditoriums to find us. Not a single housing development was located within a day's drive. (I may be exaggerating just slightly; I can't remember the exact details.)

Realizing our mistake, we promptly moved to a theater located even further from the closest homes. The auditorium was beautiful but cavernous, so no matter how many people came each weekend, each person felt like the only one there. When we moved to a smaller auditorium in the middle of a nice subdivision, the campus began to flourish.

Once we have identified the right leaders and the right location for a new campus, our third step is to find the right time. We have found that the optimum times to launch a new campus are in the fall right after school starts, at the beginning of a new year, and at Easter.

Launching the Campus

We have chosen leaders, a location, and a launch date, so now it's time to get busy with the prelaunch countdown. Successfully launching a new campus requires coordinating many different elements, and timing is essential for success. The most important elements for the successful launch of a campus include:

1. *Expansion of the leadership team.* The campus pastor now looks for a few good men, women, and teenagers. He needs leaders for the following teams: set-up and tear-down, parking, greeting, ushers, money counters (not money changers; we frown on that activity at all our campuses), and technical. Filling these roles, seeing that the leaders are trained, and helping them populate their respective teams occupies a great deal of the campus pastor's time at this stage of the launch.

2. *Purchase of equipment and supplies.* All the equipment and supplies for the campus should be on hand at least one month before the campus opens. Therefore, you need to order or borrow everything ten weeks before the launch. We try to unpack everything, set it up, and test it out at one of our existing campuses at least a month before the launch date.

   We began this testing system after discovering, on the Sunday of our first service at a new campus, that the audio snake had been shipped with the wrong connections and we couldn't plug in our sound system. We became convinced that week that a video message is less effective when the audience is forced to read lips.

3. *Establishment of a prayer base.* We may be armed with a sense of divine mission, but we are constantly aware that spiritual results do not happen without prayer. As each new campus approaches its launch day, the level of prayer likewise builds in anticipation.

Marketing the New Campus

We market our campuses in a variety of ways beginning a month before the launch. We have found through follow-up surveys that our most cost-effective marketing is signs. We put out a variety of signs every weekend at a new campus. These range from small "campaign signs" to large twenty-foot banners.

Another phase of marketing a new campus is mass mailing. We will typically send out two mailings during the two weeks before the launch of the campus. Each mailing is usually 20,000 pieces. We also run radio advertisements on secular radio stations during the two weeks before the launch, and we run newspaper ads in the weekend editions as well.

Some of our most effective marketing pieces are personal invitations. We print several hundred postcards that are similar in design to our direct-mail piece but include a space for a personal note. These are given to anyone in the launch team or in another Seacoast campus who might know a potential attendee in the new community. We ask that they write a personal invitation to their friend or relative, address the postcard, and return it to us. We then mail all the postcards. Our final marketing piece is a letter to everyone in our database who is in the new community. We invite them to attend our launch service and to consider becoming a part of the new campus.

Practice and Launch Services

Three weeks before the first official service at the new campus, we conduct our first set-up service. The goal of this first week is to get everything set up, plugged in, and tested. We then practice packing everything and putting it away.

Two weeks before the launch, we hold our second set-up service, at which we run through a typical weekend service, stopping along the way to work out the bugs. The week before the launch, we hold our official practice service. We ask the launch team to invite friends and family for a sneak preview of the new campus.

Finally, we reach launch Sunday, when we pray like crazy that someone will show up. Amazingly enough, someone always does.

Local Launch Is More Like Adding a New Service

At Seacoast, we have learned that launching a campus that is less than an hour's commute from the sponsoring campus is similar to adding a service. An area in this proximity has a built-in group of people willing to be a part of the new campus, although sometimes our job is to help them realize they are willing.

As described above, our first step in opening a new campus close to an existing campus is to identify a campus pastor. Ideally, the candidate will already be a leader in the sponsoring campus. Once identified, the leader's task is to begin building a core team, drawing from family, friends, and other contacts.

Within a few weeks of selecting a campus pastor, we invite people from the sponsoring campus to attend an informational meeting. The idea is to share the vision and invite them to become a part of the new campus. At this meeting, our goal is to recruit new leaders to work with the campus pastor and his core team.

About one month before the launch of a new campus, we have what we call a vision picnic. (In South Carolina, we're always looking for an excuse to picnic or tailgate.) We invite anyone we know who has ever attended Seacoast and lives in the new community to attend the picnic. We again share the vision for the new campus and try to give a taste of what a weekend service will be like. Our goal at the vision picnic is to begin building a crowd for launch day and to recruit volunteers for the ministry teams.

Long-Distance Launch Is More Like a Church Plant

Launching a campus that is more than an hour's commute from the original campus is more like planting a new church than starting a new service. When we plant a distance campus, we use the following four-step process, which we adapted from Dave Browning of Christ the King. These steps kick in after the campus pastor has been identified:

1. *Train the campus pastor.* Our first step is to train the new campus pastor. Each campus pastor undergoes at least three months of mentoring at the original campus before being sent to the new community. The training regimen is a mixture of classes, hands-on experience, and immersion in the Seacoast DNA.

2. *Build the core group.* The second step is to start a small group whose purpose is to build a core of leaders for the new campus. Small group members are people with Seacoast connections, their acquaintances, and people the campus pastor draws. The group meets weekly for vision casting, relationship building, and outreach.

3. *Form a worship café.* Once the core group reaches twenty to thirty adults, they move to the café stage. A medium-size space is secured for weekly celebration meetings (small church services), and the group divides into two or more small groups. The pastor continues to meet weekly with key leaders in the core group. At the weekly celebrations all the small groups come together for worship, teaching, and children's ministry.

4. *Launch the campus.* Once the core group reaches sixty to eighty committed adults, they are ready for the campus launch, which ideally will begin with 250–350 people on day one.

The preferable time period from core-group formation to campus launch is six months.

Additional Resources

Are you thinking "I've got it!" as you read this chapter? You might. Some people just need a few ideas, and they can be off and running.

Other people have "but" problems—"Yes, *but*, what about …?" You might need to make additional visits to multi-site churches, attend more multi-site training conferences,[1] and immerse yourself in some helpful books on the topic of church planting. If so, let us suggest a few books that will train you in the ABCs of church planting, using models consistent with a multi-site approach.

Churches That Multiply by Elmer Towns and Douglas Porter is a fascinating study on the book of Acts, drawing lesson after lesson about contemporary church planting. This book offers an excellent biblical foundation for church planting as an extension of the book of Acts.[2]

The Nomadic Church by Bill Easum and Pete Theodore is a worthwhile read. It contains lots of hands-on, practical advice. It covers basic stuff that any mobile church may already know, but it's an easy read for newcomers to the process and a helpful review for veterans.[3]

Starting a New Church by Dale Galloway with Warren Bird walks you through the basic steps of church planting, with an emphasis on starting as big as possible and riding as much momentum as possible.[4]

Planting New Churches in a Postmodern Age by Ed Stetzer covers a wide range of church plants, with emphasis on reaching postmodern people.[5]

Classics on church planting are *44 Questions for Church Planters* by Lyle Schaller[6] and *Church Planting for a Greater Harvest: A Comprehensive Guide* by Peter Wagner.[7]

Leadership Network's *Church-Planting Resource Guide* provides an annotated and comprehensive bibliography of general and specialty titles on church planting.[8]

• •

Workout

So how do you get this party started? Your church has determined that multi-site is the next step in fulfilling your God-given mission. You have discovered a great opportunity to expand, and the dream has been shared with the key leaders in the church. The budget has been set, and the start-up funds are in hand. Now it's time to start the countdown to launch.

In this workout, we have provided several checklists, based on a typical off-site campus in rented facilities, to help you start putting together your timeline for the launch of your off-site campus.

LAUNCH CHECKLIST

SIX MONTHS (OR MORE) BEFORE LAUNCH
- ☐ Campus pastor selected (Name) _____
- ☐ Site selected (Location)_____
- ☐ Launch date selected (Date) _____

FIVE MONTHS BEFORE LAUNCH
- ☐ Barriers, carts, miscellaneous equipment built
- ☐ Marketing material (mailers, invitations, signs, banners, etc.) created
- ☐ Core team leaders identified (see Core Team Worksheet, below)

FOUR MONTHS BEFORE LAUNCH
- ☐ Audio, lighting, and video systems ordered (or purchased)
- ☐ Signs, banners, and other marketing materials ordered
- ☐ Children's furniture/equipment purchased
- ☐ Informational meeting planned

THREE MONTHS BEFORE LAUNCH
- ☐ Informational meeting announced
- ☐ Informational meeting held
- ☐ Core teams populated (see Core Team Member Worksheet, below)

TWO MONTHS BEFORE LAUNCH
- ☐ Core-team training launched
- ☐ Vision picnic planned
- ☐ Vision picnic invitations sent

FOUR WEEKS BEFORE LAUNCH
- ☐ Vision picnic held
- ☐ Personal invitations handed out
- ☐ Set-up session 1 held on site

THREE WEEKS BEFORE LAUNCH
- ☐ Personal invitations sent
- ☐ Set-up session 2 held on site

TWO WEEKS BEFORE LAUNCH
- ☐ First mailing sent
- ☐ Preview service held

ONE WEEK BEFORE LAUNCH
- ☐ Second mailing sent

LAUNCH!

CORE TEAM LEADER WORKSHEET

Set-up Director_____

Tear-down Director _____

Worship Director_____

Children's Director _____

Small Groups Coach_____

Tech Director _____

Parking/Greeting/Ushers Director _____

CORE TEAM MEMBER WORKSHEET

SET-UP TEAM MEMBERS

_____ , _____

_____ , _____

_____ , _____

TEAR-DOWN TEAM MEMBERS

_____ , _____

_____ , _____

_____ , _____

WORSHIP TEAM MEMBERS

_____ , _____

_____ , _____

_____ , _____

CHILDREN'S TEAM LEADERS

Nursery _____

Preschool _____

Elementary _____

Tech Team_____

SMALL GROUP LEADERS

Small Group 1_____

Small Group 2_____

Small Group 3_____

Small Group 4_____

Small Group 5_____

Small Group 6_____

TECHNICAL TEAM LEADERS

Lighting _____

Audio _____

Video _____

PARKING/GREETING TEAM LEADERS

Parking_____

Greeting _____

Ushers _____

what makes

multi-site
work best

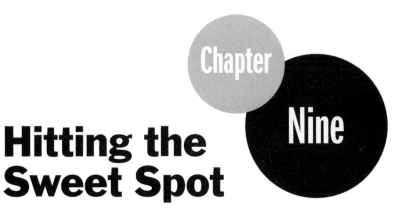

Hitting the Sweet Spot

Make sure to define and replicate your unique DNA with help from these ideas

> There is one body and one Spirit — just as you were called
> to one hope when you were called — one Lord, one faith,
> one baptism; one God and Father of all, who is over all and
> through all and in all. — EPHESIANS 4:4-6

When people in the southeastern United States think of sticky fingers, their first thought is no longer the grimy hand of a messy toddler but rather ribs and barbeque. That's because Sticky Fingers, a South Carolina – based barbeque chain, has established the reputation of having the best authentic Memphis-style ribs and barbecue in the South.

In my (Greg's) work of identifying resources to assist churches committed to multi-site, I came across this multi-unit restaurant. It seemed to face some of the same challenges multi-site churches face. After seeing a story about the growing chain on one of the national morning news shows, I picked up the phone and tracked down Jeff Goldstein, one of the founders of Sticky Fingers. I quickly learned how a lesson in running a successful barbeque restaurant could help churches understand their own DNA—that set of core beliefs and practices that must be transferred from site to site.

Jeff's insight into site selection is to go where people ask you to come. In Sticky Fingers' case, invitations are documented by the number of requests received via email. I learned his greatest insight, though, when I asked him about the source of Sticky Fingers' success. Without hesitation he responded, "Know your rib!" He went on to say that unless they have that foundational element in place, all other decisions are without consequence. The greatest location and the best staff can't cover for a poorly prepared rib.

Know Your Rib

What is your church's "rib"—your DNA? What key component(s) must be transferred from site to site, from venue to venue, to ensure the effective development of a new location? Key to replication is a clear understanding of what is foundational and what stands at the periphery.

For New Song Church in Irvine, California (stylized as NewSong), where Dave Gibbons is pastor, the church's "rib" is their vision for reconciliation. New Song, one church in four locations—Irvine, Los Angeles, and North Orange County in California, and Bangkok, Thailand—desires to be a church that releases its body to impact the world through the arts, business, and community development. New Song is about relevant and holistic ministry to the poor, technology, entrepreneurship, media, church planting, and leadership development—all with the aim of reconciling Christ and community.

This vision was born in the fall of 1993 when Dave was brokenhearted because too few churches were reaching the next generation in ways that were both postmodern and multiethnic in flavor. Dave is half Korean and half Caucasian, and as a kid, his best friends were African American or Caucasian. "I had wondered why churches were so segregated, and I saw how most churches I knew weren't connecting with my friends," he explains. "Church seemed so irrelevant and boring to them. Then I took a hard look at where I was serving. It was a great church, yet because of its immigrant nature, we weren't reaching the new global village that was fast emerging."

Everything came together for Dave one day as he read Psalm 40, which mentions a new song. "It became clear to me what the 'new song' would be," he says. "It was to begin a multiethnic or third-culture movement that would reach the next generation with a message of reconciliation."

New Song has relocated more than thirty times since its launch in 1994 with eight people in Dave's apartment. It has met in other churches, hotels, a park, a nightclub, and even the Elk's lodge. Today New Song is a dynamic and growing multiethnic church representing at least fifteen different races.

In 2001, New Song faced the inevitable: its location began to limit its ability to reach more people with the good news about Jesus. Sensing God's leading to think outside the box, New Song determined not to let land be a limitation. After exploring the options, launching a multi-site ministry seemed to be the best fit for the New Song "rib." Today multiple locations are serving to empower more people in the ministry of reconciliation as urban-suburban synergies are leveraged. Movement into diverse parts of the city of Los Angeles enabled the vision of being a multicultural church to find fuller expression. The urban-suburban synergy was also extended to an intercontinental expression: in fall 2005, New Song established a campus in Bangkok, Thailand.

Why Bangkok? Dave (whose ethnic background is Asian American, not Thai), was traveling there, and his eyes were opened to the great spiritual need and receptivity in that city. His family confirmed that call saying, "Let's go."

So in the summer of 2005, the Gibbons family moved eight thousand miles away to Bangkok, with the intention of staying there for at least a year. He remains the lead pastor of New Song Church, returning to Los Angeles every few weeks. He has developed a preaching team of about ten people in Los Angeles, and he took several people with him to Thailand—the advance team that arrived six months before the launch. His goal at that point was to identify and nurture the indigenous leadership and help them to own this site.

While the context of each New Song campus differs dramatically, the "rib" offered is the same at each: an urban-suburban synergy in which "our one-word focus is *reconciliation*," says Dave.[1]

Reproductive Necessities

Before your church reproduces itself, make sure you know what you're reproducing. Take some time to identify what you are known for—what people expect when they show up at your church. What would you identify as the reproductive necessities of your church?

Craig Groeschel, pastor of Life Church in Oklahoma City, says that for years, he and his family mapped their vacation routes to allow the maximum number of stops at Krispy Kreme doughnut stores. With the establishment of a franchise in their hometown, their vacation options have now broadened beyond the search for the neon-red "Hot Donuts" sign, but the Krispy Kreme experience frames a portion of Craig's understanding of the DNA of Life Church. He says, "The reason there is a line outside the door for forty-eight to seventy-two hours before the opening of a new store is that Krispy Kreme has created a trusted brand. You know what you will get, and you know what you get is good. We want that to be true of Life Church as well."

Lest you think this attitude smacks of consumerism, think again. Craig consistently calls people to transformed lives—consistent with Life Church's vision of turning irreligious people into fully committed followers of Jesus Christ. This vision, motivated by love for people who do not know Christ, is the foundational component of Life Church's DNA.

Guided by its vision, the DNA of Life Church is completed by a clear understanding of its core competencies—what it does best in God's kingdom:

1. Worship experiences
2. Small groups
3. Missions
4. Student ministry
5. Children's ministry

These five ministries may not seem all that dramatic, and in some sense, the list is not unusual. The important thing is that these five areas are where Life Church focuses all its resources. Thus, many of the typical ministries often found in churches, large and small alike, are not done at Life Church—women's ministry, men's ministry, recreational ministry, seniors ministry, and more. Craig and the Life team believe that although those are important ministries in the body of Christ, they are not ones that are a central part of Life Church's DNA—the role God has called Life Church to play in the kingdom.

DNA Carriers

How is a church's DNA carried from site to site and from venue to venue? The key carrier is the campus pastor or other central leaders at each campus. Greg Surratt from Seacoast Church says, "We must have a person to carry the Seacoast DNA." That someone doesn't have to have extensive training, such as a seminary degree, but that individual does have to know and embody the Seacoast "rib," whose recipe includes practical life-giving messages, a sense of God's power in worship, a relaxed nonthreatening atmosphere, excellent children's ministry, and relational small groups. The former careers of Seacoast's campus pastors include that of a dentist who now leads a campus of 1,000, a farmer who leads a campus of 600, an electrician who leads a campus of 400, and a worship leader who leads a campus of 500.

What binds other churches together? For churches that use video-cast sermons, shared teaching is often a leading factor in carrying the DNA from campus to campus, especially if sermon-based small groups reinforce the preaching. For other churches with a different in-person preacher at each site, it's the same message, as at Community Christian in Naperville, Illinois, and New Life Chicago. For churches with different on-site teachers who don't follow a mutual preaching theme, the leading DNA carrier is a common set of experiences that cause people to feel "We are one church, though in many locations."

For most churches, the DNA transfer ultimately comes down to vision and core values. The list of "must have" pieces eventually shrinks down to a handful as churches discover ways the programming may look the same or different, yet the "one church in many locations" feel is still present. For instance, the programming is almost identical at every Life Church campus. Elsewhere the programming is different—between St. Luke's in Indianapolis and the two satellite campuses, The Garden at Beef and Boards and the Garden at Oak Hill. Yet leaders at all three campuses have a strong sense of shared vision and value.

The chart on page 130 highlights the primary ways multi-site churches build their "one church" identity, according to surveys we've conducted through Leadership Network.

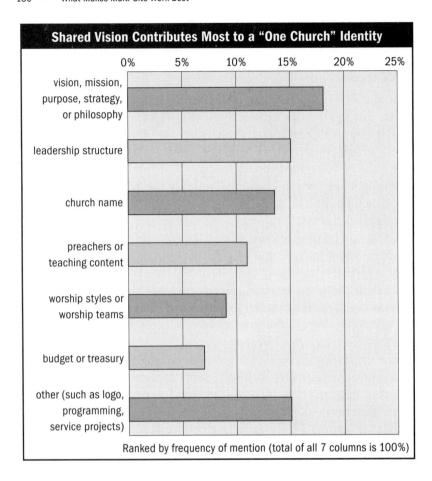

Shared Vision Contributes Most to a "One Church" Identity

Ranked by frequency of mention (total of all 7 columns is 100%)

What Type of Leader Can Best Transfer the DNA?

According to management expert Peter Drucker, no single leadership style is best for leading a healthy, growing organization, whether a church or a business. You don't even have to be born a leader; far more leaders are made than are prewired at birth.[2]

The Bible seems to affirm this idea. Look at the variety of personalities among the twelve apostles Jesus picked to spread the good news across the world. Peter was outgoing and quick to speak. Andrew, his brother, wasn't as up-front but always seemed to be finding others and bringing them along. Thomas took time to make up his mind, and

John was almost impetuous in how quickly he made decisions. Yet all became leaders of leaders—of leaders. Each person reading this book could trace back spiritually and ultimately connect with the role played by one of these twelve men in spreading the gospel.

The model in Scripture is that church leaders equip other leaders, equipping followers of Jesus for the privilege of ministry so that the body of Christ reaches full maturity (Eph. 4:11–16). In fact, church leaders build a rhythm of replication: they (1) train others (2) who train others (3) who train others (4) who train others, as the four-generation transfer is reflected in 2 Timothy 2:2. All types of people can transfer the DNA of their God-given mission to others. It is a human-to-human transfer going from heart to heart, mind to mind, spirit to spirit, and ultimately culture to culture as one campus shapes the DNA of the next campus.

Our friend Steve Yarrow, Pastor of Adult Ministries at Community Church, west of Chicago, read an early draft of this book and summarized this chapter in one sentence: "A healthy organization that overcommunicates is quintessential to driving DNA from one church campus to the next."

The Sweet Spot of Your Unique DNA

New Birth Missionary Baptist Church in Lithonia, Georgia, started as a church split—from a church split, from a church split. When Eddie Long became pastor, the environment of distrust between pastor and lay leaders was so pronounced that it took five years for the first breakthrough to occur. But he kept shaping the church's culture, defining and building unity around the distinctive purposes God had given to New Birth. Attendance grew over the years from about 200 to more than 13,000 today, and New Birth now has an influence that literally spans the globe.

Early on, Eddie realized that it is not enough to personally embody and champion the church's unique DNA; he must also replicate it through others. He began taking young leaders under his wing, investing time in them, affirming their potential, and giving them expanded opportunities for ministry. He taught his staff to do likewise.

The first waves of DNA transfer occurred within the church but soon expanded beyond its Lithonia campus. "I caught Bishop Long's spirit and the imprint of his ministry," says Andre Landers, who received Christ through the church, became a volunteer, came on staff, received extensive mentoring, and led what became a church plant, New Birth South Metropolitan Church.

The next waves took the approach of one church in multiple locations. One of the early out-of-state New Birth campuses is in Charlotte, North Carolina, where Eddie Long grew up and maintained many connections over the years. The founding pastor there, Terrell Murphy, is now mentoring those who will start New Birth campuses in other cities. He explains, "We're an extension of what's inside Bishop Long. As Isaac built on things inside Abraham's heart, we are sons and daughters who have joined our hearts to his, as our people are to us, which allows us to build generationally on the path Bishop Long has set."

Indeed, part of New Birth's success is its environment of constantly seeking a "sweet spot" in how to transfer its DNA across the unfolding New Birth movement.

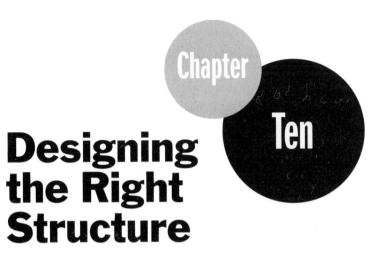

Designing the Right Structure

Learn to grow at multiple locations by modifying the way you staff, structure, and communicate

> Moses' father-in-law replied, "What you are doing is not good. You and these people who come to you will only wear yourselves out. The work is too heavy for you; you cannot handle it alone." — EXODUS 18:17 - 18

In 1992, I (Geoff) was elected to become senior pastor of a small-town Texas church by a vote of eleven for, one against, and one abstention. (The vote represented every adult in the church. The lady who abstained later told me that she didn't know me well enough to cast a ballot at that time. After getting to know me, she quit the church.) One of my first tasks as pastor was to lay out an organizational chart. It looked like the chart on page 134.

This was the best organization I had ever worked for. Communication flowed freely, staff meetings were always well attended, and there was very little political infighting.

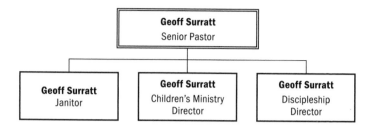

The capacity of this organization, however, was somewhat limited. As the church grew, the organization had to grow and change with it, but the basic structure remained very simple.

When I came to Seacoast Church in 1996, it had 1,000 weekend attendees and thirty full-time staff members, but the organization was very similar to the one I had left in Texas. As the church grew and people were added, we simply added more boxes and levels of administration. Communication became more challenging, but the lines of responsibility were very clear. This basic structure served us well until we began to add campuses.

Soon after adding our second off-site campus, it became apparent that we would need to find a new paradigm for structure. We began to think in terms of being an organism more than being an organization and looked for ways to connect based more on job description and relationship rather than on hierarchy. Now, four years after opening our first off-site campus, we have nine campuses in seven cities across two states. Our structure bears little resemblance to the neat chart I first created fourteen years ago.

As a church considers adding an off-site campus, the first questions church leaders ask are:

- How will this affect our organization?
- Who will answer to whom?
- Who will be responsible for the content and quality of the services at the new location?
- How will we make sure everyone is on the same page?

In raising these questions, leaders are seeking a clearer picture of what their new multi-site campus relationships will look like. As they answer the questions, they begin making adjustments to the organization of the church. As they do so, chances are they will go through three stages of organizational changes.

Stage 1: One Off-Site Campus

While a church's decision to open its first off-site campus is often the toughest part of becoming a multi-site church, opening its first additional site doesn't normally require a great deal of change to the church's overall structure. A church will often treat its first new site as just another ministry of the original campus, much like the children's ministry or youth ministry. Department leaders will usually report directly to the ministry leader at the original campus rather than to the campus pastor. The new site will look and feel like the original campus as much as possible. Communication becomes very crucial at this stage, but overseeing the new site with existing staff is manageable.

Stage 2: Two to Three Off-Site Campuses

As a second or third off-site campus is added, the traditional church structure begins to sag. Now, for instance, the children's ministry leader at the original campus has to oversee weekend services at the original campus (which was a full-time job to begin with), give leadership to two additional children's ministry directors, and find time to visit the other campuses. The children's ministry leader begins to be stressed out, and all the campuses suffer.

You know it's time to restructure when just the mention of adding a third campus causes a staff member to run crying from the room. (If the men's ministry director is crying, you may have waited too long.)

The first significant change for a church in stage 2 is often the transition from part-time to full-time campus pastors for the off-site locations. When Life Church in Oklahoma City added its first two campuses, two members of its executive team took on the additional role of campus pastor. As the campuses grew and their vision began to expand, they soon saw the need for full-time leaders at each campus. They began training apprentice leaders at each campus and, over a period of months, turned the day-to-day operations over to these new leaders.

Another change that often happens in stage 2 is that an overall multi-site director is selected. This is often a senior-level staff member who has helped get the first two or three campuses off the ground.

Multi-site directors are to wake up every morning thinking about the off-site campuses and then go to bed dreaming of the next site.

After Seacoast opened its first off-site campus, the pastor of a church we had helped start four years earlier approached us about becoming a campus rather than being an independent church. This presented several challenges: the church was one hundred miles from our original campus, we would have to make major changes to the style and structure of the new campus, and our staff was already feeling the burn from the campus we had started two months earlier.

> Multi-site directors are to wake up every morning thinking about the off-site campuses and then go to bed dreaming of the next site.

We made two strategic decisions at that point. First, we enlisted the help of Byron Davis, the former CEO of Fisher Price Toys, who had retired in Charleston and attended our church. Second, my responsibilities were reshuffled so that my primary concern became starting and overseeing new campuses. Byron and I began meeting weekly to strategize and plan how we could fulfill the vision of becoming one church, many campuses. Because I was freed up to focus on opening campuses as Seacoast's multi-site director, we were able to move very quickly, going from one campus to nine in less than three years.

A third change for churches in stage 2 is the addition of a campus pastor at the original site. The senior pastor no longer has the luxury of focusing solely on that location but must cast vision for the entire church body. As a result, someone needs to oversee the original campus in a similar fashion to each of the multi-sites. At Community Christian Church in Chicago, Dave Ferguson is the lead pastor, but Troy McMahon is the campus pastor of the original campus. Dave focuses on the big picture, the overall vision of the church, while Troy oversees the staff and ministry at the largest campus. Most multi-site churches in stage 2 quickly discover the need for a campus pastor in addition to the lead pastor at the original campus.

At this point, churches begin to use terms like "vertical accountability" and "horizontal relationships with solid or dotted line connections." (Consultants *love* this stuff.) What they mean is that the staff at an off-site campus is accountable to a campus pastor for job performance, ministry effectiveness, and the staff responsibilities within that campus. At the same time, staff members will be on a ministry-specific team (youth ministry, media ministry, etc.) with their counterparts at the other campuses. One of the campus leaders (often the leader at the original campus) will act as team leader. These cross-campus teams focus on decisions and projects that affect every campus.

To better understand the organization of a multi-site church in stage 2, let's look at the mythical First Church of Perpetual Illustrations. First Church has four campuses: the original campus, off-site one, off-site two, and off-site tres (a cross-cultural campus). At off-site one, Shepherd Sue is the campus pastor, and Crazy Al is the youth director. Crazy Al is also on the First Church youth ministry team along with the youth directors at every campus.

When Crazy Al takes nine teenagers to summer camp but comes back with only seven, it is Shepherd Sue's job to sit down with Crazy Al and explain to him in Christian love that if he ever does that again, he will be posting his resume at ChurchStaffing.com. When Crazy Al decides he wants to teach only from Leviticus for the next three years because his teens need to "dive deep in the Word," he takes the idea to the youth ministry team. The leader of that team, Mature Bob, tells Crazy Al that this is not in keeping with the philosophy of youth ministry at First Church, affirming that Crazy Al needs to stick with the curriculum that all the other campuses are using.

When Crazy Al tells Mature Bob that he's going to teach Leviticus anyway because he's seen a vision in the fungus growing in his bathroom, Mature Bob shares his concerns with Shepherd Sue. Shepherd Sue then sits down with Crazy Al and helps him polish his resume for his next phase of ministry. The organizational chart at First Church looks like this:

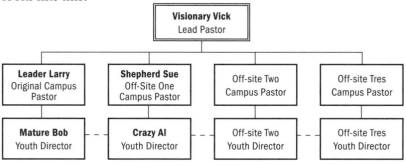

Stage 3: Four or More Campuses

Adding campuses is similar to having children. Having one child doesn't require a major change in lifestyle for most couples. Sure, they have to hire a babysitter to have date nights, and they can't remember the last time they had a good night's sleep, but things are still relatively simple. Adding a second child seems to quadruple the challenges, and adding a third child raises the level of family complexity exponentially. Families with four or more children, however, seem to find a system that accommodates the additional offspring with minimal upset to the core. That's the goal of a multi-site church as it moves from being an organization to being an organism: to accommodate growth without having to reinvent the structure.

When Oklahoma's Life Church added its fourth campus in Stillwater, it became apparent to the church leaders that they needed some form of central services that would support all the campuses. They decided to move to a completely different structure from the one they had used to grow to date. They put a small staff at each campus to focus on the needs of that specific site and moved everyone else to central support to focus on the needs of Life Church as a whole. Since reorganizing, the church has grown from 7,000 to over 14,000 weekend attendees and has opened additional sites, including satellites in the East Valley section of Phoenix (see story in chapter 1).

> That's the goal of a multi-site church as it moves from being an organization to being an organism: to accommodate growth without having to reinvent the structure.

Seacoast Church faced a similar challenge as we (Geoff) contemplated a vision to have almost twenty sites within a very few years. The original campus felt bombarded by the needs and requests of all the off-site campuses, and the campuses felt like they were being ignored. So Seacoast followed Life Church's example and built a central-support group to service the needs at all the campuses. We organized central support into three areas: business operations, leadership development, and campus operations. This has given us the ability to continue to add campuses without draining the resources of the original site.

Communication

Once you branch out beyond one site, communication among staff and volunteer leaders can become a major challenge. Calling an all-staff meeting now involves travel arrangements and coordinating the schedules across several individual staffs. When an assistant at the Charleston campus of Seacoast Church sent out an all-staff notice announcing that the new trash cans had arrived and could be picked up at the front desk, staff members two hundred miles away in Greenville and Savannah wrote back asking if they really had to drive three hours just to pick up trash cans. Multi-site churches must become very creative in keeping everyone on the same page. Some of the tools churches have used to accomplish this include:

Intranet Site

Seacoast now uses an intranet site designed for staff members only, which allows them to share documents and information. Several online discussions are always in progress as the staff share ideas for upcoming series, brainstorm ideas for more effective volunteer recruitment, and create better procedures for tracking attendance.

Blogs

Several multi-site churches have created online blogs (short for web log, a simple Internet site that can be easily updated) to keep church members and staff up to date with what is happening churchwide. Blogs are a great way to share ideas, disseminate information, and collaborate without adding another meeting to the schedule. Team members can read new information or contribute data or ideas whenever they have time and wherever they have Internet access. At campuses that rely mostly on volunteer staff, this kind of open access is invaluable.

At Seacoast, we too have found blogs to be a great way for our campuses to communicate with their own congregations. Each campus can quickly upload its own events, news, and devotionals. All our blogs are linked to the main Seacoast blog (www.seacoastchurch.typepad. com), and many staff members have their own blogs (mine is www. geoffsurratt.typepad.com).

Videoconferences and Teleconferences

While not ideal, teleconferences can be a great tool for connecting a diverse staff located on multiple campuses. Seacoast uses a weekly teleconference to connect all the campus pastors. Pastors share what is happening on their campuses, how the past weekend went, and any upcoming events that might be of interest to other campuses. The senior pastor participates in the conference to connect with all the pastors and to share vision and direction for the future. While the teleconferences can never replace the need for face-to-face meetings, they do help keep a sense of connection and unity among the campuses.

Community Christian Church in Chicago uses videoconferences and teleconferences to connect its partners located in different parts of the country. They meet weekly to collaborate on the weekend message, focus on upcoming concerns, and enhance the sense of community. This allows each partner to leverage the creativity and insight of the entire team on their individual locations. As previously mentioned, Community Christian meets every Tuesday in a videoconference with their partner churches to collaboratively build their content for upcoming series.

The Myth of Cloning

A multi-site church is a diverse organization with a wide variety of needs. The original campus is often an established church with a staff geared to meet the needs of that congregation. New campuses present new challenges.

Paul and Barnabas discovered some of the organizational challenges of a multi-campus church very early on, as reflected in Acts 15. The Jerusalem campus felt that the other congregations just weren't doing things the way they were done at the "main campus," so several self-appointed leaders headed to Antioch to straighten them out. "This brought Paul and Barnabas into sharp dispute and debate with them" (Acts 15:2). Paul and Barnabas were appointed, along with some other church members, to go to Jerusalem to sort out this problem. At Jerusalem, they began working out organizational challenges, defining the essential DNA of the new church, and clarifying how best to communicate between the campuses.

The early church soon came to reflect the perspective that the needs of a congregation twenty miles away are different from the needs in the original community. The dynamics of a small campus are different than those of a large church. The new campuses are likely filled with people who are unfamiliar with the standard operating procedures of the original campus. And as seasoned staff members are moved to new sites, the original campus can be drained of the experienced and talented staff it once had.

> The early church soon came to reflect the perspective that the needs of a congregation twenty miles away are different from the needs in the original community.

Because of these factors, it is important that a multi-site church be structured more like an organism than like an organization; the structure will have to morph and change rapidly as the dynamics of new campuses are brought into the picture. So how do you structure an organism rather than an organization? You can't; you can only grow an organism, and you grow an organism by growing leaders. We'll look at the process in chapter 11.

Building Better Leaders

Experience success by emphasizing the role of campus pastors, developing the next generation of leaders, and promoting from within

So, my son, throw yourself into this work for Christ. Pass on what you heard from me – the whole congregation saying Amen! – to reliable leaders who are competent to teach others."

— 2 TIMOTHY 2:1 - 2 MESSAGE

Moses' congregation was out of control. It had started simply enough, Moses heard a clear call from a burning bush to lead God's people to a new place. He knew his mission. His vision was clear: lead the children of Israel from bondage to freedom, from the land of slavery to the land of promise.

This stuff would preach. Moses' new work got off to a great start, doubling when Moses recruited his brother Aaron. It still seemed manageable growing another 50 percent when their sister Miriam got on board.

Moses felt comfortable with "we three and no more," but that's when things started to get out of hand. As God began to use Moses in spectacular ways, the "church" grew to over one million people in a few short months, and Moses was way behind the curve in adding new staff. In fact, his only staff was a stick that occasionally turned into a snake. (A trick many a church staff would repeat in the future!)

One day Moses' father-in-law and mentor, Jethro, came for a visit to see how the exodus was going. He saw that Moses was overwhelmed, the people weren't being cared for, and the newly formed nation was coming apart at the seams. He gave Moses some excellent advice:

> Select capable men from all the people — men who fear God, trustworthy men who hate dishonest gain — and appoint them as officials over thousands, hundreds, fifties and tens. Have them serve as judges for the people at all times, but have them bring every difficult case to you; the simple cases they can decide themselves. That will make your load lighter, because they will share it with you. If you do this and God so commands, you will be able to stand the strain, and all these people will go home satisfied.
>
> EXODUS 18:21–23

Moses saw the wisdom in his father-in-law's advice. He broke the nation of Israel into small groups and community-size groups, and he commissioned leaders over them. He continued to be the primary vision caster and the one ultimately responsible for the direction of the children of Israel, but he entrusted the day-to-day care and feeding of the people to trusted leaders. You might say that Moses created the first multi-site church.

You might say that Moses created the first multi-site church.

The key to success for Moses' multi-site effort is the same key for any multi-site church today: leadership development. Finding, training, and deploying effective leaders are the keys to successfully building a church in more than one location. It seems simple, but people often underestimate the importance of leadership in building off-site campuses.

It's easy to see the spectacular lighting, hear the incredible audio, experience the lifelike video at a campus like Fellowship Church in Texas or Life Church in Oklahoma, and think technology is the primary explanation. Or to be swept up in the excellence of the music at North Point's Buckhead campus, the drama at Willow Creek, or the creative teaching at Community Christian and believe that all a church needs to do is to reproduce those elements of the weekend experience and they will automatically see success.

Moses' congregation had great lights, sound, and video, incredible music, and very creative teaching tools — ranging from a pillar of fire, the voice of God, and first-edition stone copies of the Ten Commandments. But the bottom line for success was leaders who followed God. Every successful multi-site church would say the same: technology, creativity, and excellence are all window dressing compared to discovering, developing, and deploying effective leaders.

What Leaders Do We Need for Our Next Campus?

While different multi-site churches handle staffing with a great variety of approaches, several leadership roles are common to almost all successful models.

1. *Multi-Site Director.* This is the person who is responsible for daily steering the multi-site mission. Sometimes this is the first person a church hires as it considers adding off-site campuses, but often the need for this position emerges over time. As a second, third, and fourth campus is added, the need for someone to oversee this part of the church's ministry becomes very apparent.

2. *Campus Pastor.* The key to any new start-up is the campus pastor. This is the leader who will convey the DNA of the primary campus, recruit the core team, develop the new leaders, and carry on the ministry once the campus is launched.

   Churches with experience in developing campus pastors told us they look for these qualities:

Top Five Campus-Pastor Qualities

- A leader who completely buys into the church's vision and is loyal to its senior leadership
- A team player with strong relational skills
- A team builder who can reproduce vision in others
- A pastor, someone with a desire and heart to shepherd groups and individuals
- A flexible entrepreneur

3. *Worship Director.* In addition to the campus pastor, the worship director oversees the weekend experience at the new campus. This person is responsible for creating an authentic worship experience that reflects the atmosphere of the primary campus.

4. *Children/Youth Ministry Director.* After the quality of the overall weekend experience, the quality of the ministry to children often determines the success or failure of a new campus. Similar to the role of the worship director, the leaders in children's ministry strive to replicate as much as possible the environment of the primary campus.

5. *Small Groups/Spiritual Life/Discipleship Director.* Often a volunteer in the beginning, this director is responsible for the spiritual development programs and ministries of the new campus.

Ten Practical Ideas for Leadership Development

Obviously, many more leaders are needed to successfully launch a new campus. How will you find and develop all the necessary leaders? Here are ten practical ideas for leadership development in a multi-site church.

1. *Remember that most leaders are already present; they can be raised up from within the congregation.* Some churches have found success in bringing in outside leaders to grow their new campuses. They have brought in newly graduated seminary students, staff members from other churches, or senior pastors who feel a need to change direction in their ministry. Willow Creek launched its regional ministry by first bringing in Jim Tomberlin, who had built a very successful church in Colorado Springs. Jim built the core team for the first campus launch, oversaw the hiring of new staff, and mentored the campus pastor, who eventually took over the ministry. By bringing in an entrepreneurial leader with a great deal of experience, Willow was able to get their first regional campus up and running in a relatively short amount of time.

The most common advice from seasoned leader-making churches, however, is to raise the leaders you need from within your congregation. There are several advantages to this approach. First, one of the key components to building a church that meets in more than one location is the ability to replicate the vision, the core values, and the heart of the church (its DNA). Passing on the heart of a ministry to someone who has not been a part of forming that heart and has not experienced the blood, sweat, and tears of building that ministry is a very difficult process. The challenge comes when an outside leader who lacks the basic DNA of a church then leads a campus of that church: misunderstandings, conflict, and resentment can arise.

Another advantage churches have found in raising up new multi-site leadership from within is that the new leader is already a part of the strong culture of that church. In growing churches, the culture can become so strong that it is almost cultlike and can be very difficult to break into. While everyone smiles at newcomers, shows them how to use the copy machine, and assures them how excited the church is to have them on board, they're still not accepted as "one of us." Jim Collins describes this type of culture in his book *Built to Last*: "Working at a visionary company is almost like joining a cult. There is generally a feeling of elitism and an almost fanatical loyalty among the long-term staff members. It's the corporate equivalent of belonging to the U.S. Marine Corps. You either shape up or ship out."

> The most common advice from seasoned leader-making churches, however, is to raise the leaders you need from within your congregation.

This strong culture manifests itself in strong ties among staff members who have a revolutionary outlook of taking on the world for God. Unfortunately, that culture can also reject leadership that comes in from the outside.

Because of the challenges of bringing in outside leadership, many multi-site churches look to promote from within. The first place they look is to leaders already on staff. When opening a first off-site campus, churches will often simply add oversight of the campus to the already bulging portfolio of a high-capacity staff member. When the campus grows to a point where it obviously needs a full-time leader, either that staff member or someone he has mentored will be given that responsibility. As campuses are added, this process is often repeated with other staff members. The challenge is that eventually the primary site will be drained of its best and brightest leaders. As the new campuses experience the excitement of new growth, the original site begins to feel stagnant. Eventually new leadership must be developed.

Few people represent that ideal better than Mark Jobe, pastor of New Life Community Church, an urban Chicago congregation that today meets at eight satellite locations every Sunday. When the church initially began growing, Mark hoped to hire additional leaders, but he couldn't find anyone willing to move to his tough, southwest Chicago neighborhood. He felt his only choice was to develop leaders from the people the church had.

> He looked for people who matched the qualities of the acronym FAST — people who were faithful, available, Spirit-filled, and teachable.

"My first leadership team consisted of four unlikely candidates — a young Hispanic man fresh out of the Marines, two gypsy brothers, and a former alcoholic who came to Christ in his sixties," Mark told *Leadership Journal*. "None of them had any biblical training for leadership. None had ever led in a church setting before."[1]

His strategy was simple: he looked for people who matched the qualities of the acronym FAST — people who were *f*aithful, *a*vailable, Spirit-filled, and *t*eachable. Then he would follow the example of how Jesus apprenticed his disciples, by building a highly relational, hands-on team. Mark met weekly with his leadership team to pray, learn, discuss, and most importantly, to develop friendships. This group, initially all men, had fun together and grew close, and so did their wives.

"At almost every point of ministry, I found some way to include one of the people we were apprenticing," Mark says. "As the church grew, we created more entry points of leadership so that more people could be apprenticed."

> "As the church grew, we created more entry points of leadership so that more people could be apprenticed."
> — Mark Jobe

As church attendance grew from 20 to some 2,600 today, Mark trained pastors for each of the satellite locations. "All but one of those pastors was grown from within our church," he says. Eighteen years later, one of his original "four unlikely candidates" is still a pastor, serving alongside Mark today. John Palmieri, one of New Life Chicago's longtime satellite pastors, adds, "We still choose 'unlikely candidates,' and over time they usually turn out to be our most effective shepherds!"

If the trend is toward homegrown staff, then what about the role of formal education for ministry, such as Bible school or seminary? A few larger churches have developed a formal partnership with a Christian school of higher education and incorporate the school's training into their own programming. An increasing number of churches are also encouraging the use of distance education, such as satellite campuses, modular training, or online classes.

Questions That Help You Spot New Leaders

How do you identify people who are capable of learning leadership? Fred Smith Sr. (www.breakfastwithfred.com), a columnist for *Leadership Journal*, mapped out eight signs of leadership potential. Looking for these signs will help you discern which people are capable of learning to lead, including people without a proven track record whom you're considering for a leadership position.

1. *Do I see a constructive spirit of discontent?* The person who observes, "There's got to be a better way to do this," is probably a leader. People locked inside the *status quo* are not leaders.
2. *Do they offer practical ideas?* Leaders seem able to identify which ideas are practical and which aren't.
3. *Is anybody listening?* When leaders speak, people listen. If nobody listens to them, they're not giving leadership.
4. *Does anyone respect them?* If people respect a person, they'll follow that person.
5. *Can they create or catch vision?* When they talk to people about the future, do their hearers' eyes light up? A person who doesn't feel the thrill of challenge is not a potential leader.
6. *Do they show a willingness to take responsibility?* Potential leaders accept the pressures of responsibility. They sense that the joy of contributing to other people is what leadership is all about.
7. *Do they finish the job?* The person who grabs hold of a problem and won't let go, like a dog with a bone, usually has leadership potential.
8. *Are they tough-minded?* No one can lead without being criticized or without facing discouragement.[2]

At Seacoast, all ministry training classes are being offered online through the Online Learning initiative led by Mac Lake, the leadership development pastor. The goal is for anyone at anytime to have access to the educational tools they need to become a leader at Seacoast.

2. *Use small groups to develop leaders.* If future church leaders are already present but untapped, is there a specific way they can be surfaced? In *Nine Keys to Effective Small-Group Leadership*, Carl George says that the small group is, "from a leadership-development standpoint, the best possible laboratory" for identifying and training the next generation of volunteer leaders.[3] "The central leadership task of the church, after hearing from God, is to develop leaders,"[4] he affirms.

We made a similar confirmation through a 2003 survey of Leadership Network's Multi-Site Churches Leadership Communities. Asked to respond to a series of statements about leadership development, 80 percent of survey respondents agreed that small group leadership plays an essential training role (see chart on p. 150).

Typical is New Life Chicago. "Home groups are our main focus for leadership development," says John Palmieri. "We call our pipeline a leadership farm system." It works like this:

1. New believers are placed in a mentoring relationship
2. Next possible step: apprentice in home group
3. Next possible step: home group leader
4. Next possible step: team leader over a couple of groups
5. Next possible step: pastoral internship for one year of pastoral training

The same idea works for small service groups and even for small groups that travel. Jeff Brodie, youth pastor at Chartwell Baptist Church, says "Our best practice to develop leaders is sending people on short-term mission trips."

The strong connection between small groups and leadership development causes some churches to evaluate the implications of that link for launching new campuses. "We are finding it best for the campus pastor also to oversee the small groups for that campus. The campus pastor can leverage his influence and visibility to enlist new small group leaders as well as to encourage newcomers to get connected in small groups," says Jon Ferguson, community pastor at Community Christian Church in Chicago.

By the time Seacoast was ready to open its sixth campus, we (Geoff) knew we couldn't afford to drain any more talent from the existing staff, so we turned to our small group system to find our next campus pastor. Phil Strange was the ideal candidate. Phil had committed his life to Christ at Seacoast several years earlier. His first place of ministry had been working in the parking ministry on the weekends. He soon started volunteering with his wife, Sherry, in the nursery. Eventually someone invited Phil and Sherry to attend their small group, and Phil became the worship leader because he was the one who knew how

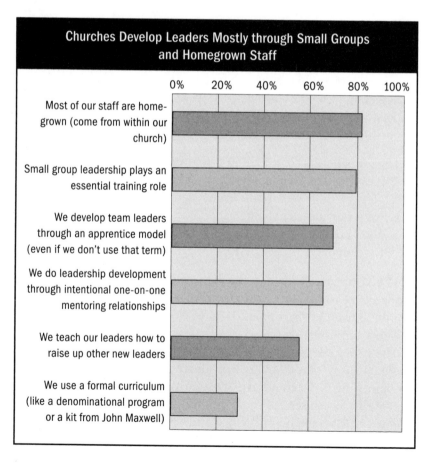

Churches Develop Leaders Mostly through Small Groups and Homegrown Staff

	0%	20%	40%	60%	80%	100%
Most of our staff are homegrown (come from within our church)						
Small group leadership plays an essential training role						
We develop team leaders through an apprentice model (even if we don't use that term)						
We do leadership development through intentional one-on-one mentoring relationships						
We teach our leaders how to raise up other new leaders						
We use a formal curriculum (like a denominational program or a kit from John Maxwell)						

to play the guitar. When the group divided, Phil and Sherry led the new group, and a few months later, they were asked to coach several small group leaders. Phil had never been to seminary, had never given a sermon, had never performed a wedding, baptism, or funeral, but he was the ideal candidate for a campus pastor. Beyond meeting the biblical qualifications for an elder, Phil was a proven leader, he had the Seacoast DNA, and the culture was already engrained in him. All he needed was a little on-the-job training, some basic theological and pastoral instruction, and a lot of support. His campus launched three months after he came on staff and grew to over 500 people within the first year. Many multi-site churches find their ideal campus leaders already serving in their small group ministries.

3. *Remember that leadership development is more relational than anything else.* One error that churches often make when looking at leadership development is to mistake a program or a class with building leaders. When Jesus developed the twelve men to whom he would entrust the most important mission of history, he didn't send them to a class or put them through a program. Jesus developed his leaders by hanging out with them, eating with them, and experiencing life with them. As churches begin to expand rapidly through multiple campuses, it's important to remember that the most effective means of leadership development is sitting around a dinner table, sharing the ups and downs of life.

The experience of Community Christian Church in Chicago proves that relational leadership development can be done long distance. "Every Tuesday morning since 2001, we have videoconferenced with a church we're apprenticing in Denver, Colorado," says Dave Ferguson, lead pastor. Those experiences worked so well that four more apprentice churches—in Bakersfield (California), Detroit, Boston, and Manhattan—have joined the weekly video-conference sessions.

On Tuesday afternoons at Community Christian, the teaching teams from all locations collaborate long-distance on various parts of service planning. They work on everything from the message for that week to programming. The leadership development occurs as if

> "Every Tuesday morning since 2001, we have videoconferenced with a church we're apprenticing in Denver."
>
> — Dave Ferguson

everyone were in the same room, but in reality some are almost two thousand miles away!

"The determining factor isn't geographical, but relational."
– Eric Bramlett

As Community Christian partners with other churches, geographical distance has become a non-issue. "Multi-site is not about geography; it is about relationships," says Dave Ferguson. "The determining factor isn't geographical, but relational," summarizes Eric Bramlett, who has served since 1996 as creative arts director at Community Christian.

4. *Look at leadership development from the new leader's point of view.*

- View from one side of the fence: "Our new site or venue has quickly become part of our DNA for how we do church."
- View from the other side of the fence: "Our newest extension is like a virus — it's a disease that eats into our best resources."

In the first view, new or developing leaders have a sense of fulfillment. In the second view, they feel used, unappreciated, or even cut off from the whole. The implication is what one multiple-campus pastor observed: "You may think your sites to be part of the DNA, but others view them as a virus!"

A case in point is Grace Community Church in Tyler, Texas, which runs five services weekly on three different campuses. The church sent out a staff couple to another campus. This couple had been heavily involved with children's ministries. When the couple left, there was a temporary but predictable shake-up and drop in the quality of children's programming, raising concerns for certain parents. The couple went off being told they were vanguards, but they soon heard rumblings from the group they left, equating them with an energy-robbing virus.

"That's one of the hidden costs of multi-site," says Gary Brandenburg, senior pastor at the time. "When you send key staff members to carry the DNA to another location, unless you're real careful, they leave a temporary vortex of turbulence, which must be addressed and settled before you can move forward."

Sometimes the opposite happens. Sometimes the new leader feels affirmed and empowered to the point that myopia sets in. Sometimes these leaders become so intent on following opportunity that they don't notice the costs of their decision back at the home base. Many churches, for example, can tell a story of a talented lay leader or staff pastor with a growing ministry that the rest of the church supports with prayer, energy, resources, and collaboration. Then one day, this arm of the church decides to go it alone—perhaps becoming a separate church or affiliating with another church.

"That happened to us recently," commented one member of a Leadership Network Multi-site Churches Leadership Community. "When they opted to follow their dream, they didn't see the huge unintended consequences for the rest of us, such as loss of home-base energy and diffusion of our resources." This particular church, which has long warned against the "silo mentalities" of doing ministry without regard for other departments of the church, would still rather have taken the hit than not have risked at all.

5. *Check for alignment of implicit and explicit values.* Sometimes a question comes along that stops you cold. Tim Lundy, directional leader at Fellowship Bible Church, couldn't let go of this thought: "Are we doing multi-site as one of the programs of our church, or are we a multi-site church?" The answer helped him define his church's identity. It also helped pinpoint his commitment level to leadership development. "For me personally, the question helped narrow what I need to be doing in leadership development—and also what I need to stop doing," he says. Tim is now more intentional about leadership development because he sees his church differently.

> "Are we doing multi-site as one of the programs of our church, or are we a multi-site church?"
> —Tim Lundy

Kevin Penry, pastor of multi-campus development at Life Church in Oklahoma City made a similar discovery. "I got to thinking about the difference between multi-site as something we *do* versus multi-site as who we *are*," he says. "An alignment of our implicit and explicit values happens best when multi-site is something we *are*."

David Dotlich, coauthor with James Noel of *Action Learning: How the World's Top Companies Are Re-Creating Their Leaders and Themselves*, says that the strength and depth of a leadership talent pool predicts the success of an organization, including a church.[5] "Every organization has an 'implicit' process for replicating leadership," he told us. One way to tell whether your leadership model is the right one is, according to David, by asking "Who gets ahead?" That is, "Who gets rewarded and moves forward?"

David also emphasizes the changes needed in leaders' roles. "Each passage in the leadership pipeline requires new learnings and behaviors," he says. He maps out a cumulative series of management skills that are needed to keep the leadership pipeline from clogging:

- Level-one leaders are most successful when they learn to delegate — to share ministry with others.
- Level-two leaders (analogous to middle management in the business world) know both how to manage people and how to allocate resources.
- Level-three leaders (functional management) learn how to grow others by taking them through the right experiences.
- Level-four leaders develop a strategy for an entire ministry (function or business), such as a church satellite campus.
- Level-five leaders learn how to work as a team of leaders.
- Level-six leaders (equivalent to a business CEO) ask questions about how to service prospective and existing "customers," which for a church translates into questions of how best to reach and serve those whom God is calling.

"Leadership cannot be bought: it must be built," David summarizes, "by leaders who develop other leaders." Therefore, he suggests, if leaders aren't the people who get ahead, and if you're not turning out enough leaders, you might have a vision-alignment problem. "Your leadership practices and culture may reflect what you did in the past but not what you need for the future," he says.

6. Set up simple ways to measure leadership development, and more of it will happen. The old saying is right: "What gets measured gets done." In biblical terms, we reap what we sow, as Galatians 6:8 and 2 Corinthians 9:6 affirm.

Dave Browning, of Christ the King Community Church in Mount Vernon, Washington, says, "We have discovered in fact, we are not so much about multiplying campuses as we are about multiplying lead-

Developing New Leaders				
Christ the King Community Church (CTK), Mount Vernon, WA, www.ctkonline.com				
Step	**1**	**2**	**3**	**4**	**5**
We	Identify	Recruit	Deploy	Train	Support
They	Go through orientation process (through www.ctkon line.com)	Enroll in training (through the online CTK University)	Lead a group (register it online)	Direct a video café (apply online to affiliate it with CTK USA)	Pastor a worship center (coordinate through CTK Central Services)

ers. As you multiply leaders, you need more places for them to lead, and therefore more campuses." Christ the King has established two processes for measuring leadership development. One is for developing new leaders (p. 155), and the other is for moving someone from volunteer to full-time vocational work (p. 156). Each process involves a set of staff roles that can be adapted at the church's off-site locations but can also be reproduced in almost limitless contexts, such as by other affiliated churches across the country or world as they are developed.

> "We have discovered in fact, we are not so much about multiplying campuses as we are about multiplying leaders."
> — Dave Browning

How does that happen? Christ the King leverages the Internet, using an online strategy and DVDs as training tools that can be used anywhere. "The goal is to carry the informational content—about 70 percent of training—as much as possible through the Web and DVD, so that we don't have to be limited by geography," says Dave. "The relational content—about 30 percent of the training—will be personal. Touch points will be to talk about the content they've gone over."

The Internet materials also serve as a prescreening process to help leaders find people whose passions and values have a potential match with what Christ the King is doing. "It's a mechanism for assimilating

				Entrepreneurial Career Path	

Context	Size	Relationships Impacted	Process	Training Focus	Leadership Role
Individual	1	Person	Enroll in CTK University	Culture, leadership, organization	Initiator (volunteer)
Small group	1 – 10	Person, friends	Register group online with Ixthus	Groups, people, discipleship	Facilitator (volunteer)
Video café	10 – 50	Person, friends, groups	Apply to CTK USA	Worship, operations, publicity	Director (bi-vocational)
Worship center	50 – 500	Person, friends, groups, café	Inform CTK Central Services	Teaching, children, youth	Pastor (vocational)

Christ the King Community Church, Mount Vernon, WA, www.ctkonline.com

the right sorts of people into our culture," says Dave. "We want their mission, vision, and values to intersect with ours, and until we know that's going to happen, we don't get too excited."

With simple tools like these, leaders at Christ the King can identify where someone is in the leadership development process, what measurable outcomes should be anticipated, and what the next stage will be in a leader's developmental progression.

7. Develop leaders by organizing teams that are specific to each campus or venue. Life Church in Oklahoma City formed in 1996. As the result of a merger of two different congregations, it became multi-site in 2001, and by early 2004, it was holding twelve services a week on four campuses, built around video and television venues.

The church's evangelistic vision involves being one church with multiple locations. The rapid growth and multiple worship services require a flexible staff and a steady stream of new leaders. Initially the church built leadership teams and structures as if its multi-campus approach had no bearing.

Then in 2003 church leaders made an important discovery. "Our challenge was to make our staff look like the vision, because it didn't," says Sam Roberts, pastor of creative media. "So we reorganized the staff teams specific to each campus. That has brought focus to our staff, easily making them twice as effective as they were."

Now, with most staff members focused on the congregation and outreach of one specific location, each campus has a strong sense of ownership. "Life Church is blessed to have come upon the leadership structure we now have," says Kevin Penry, pastor of multi-campus development. "It allows us to move better toward our objectives."

This process of staff realignment sometimes requires the creation of new centralized staff roles as well, such as Kevin's position. In other churches, a whole system of new roles sometimes needs to be created. Some of Life Church's new roles are site specific, and others are coordination related.

8. Explore the attitude of interdependence. Willow Creek Community Church, in northwest suburban Chicago, launched a regional-campus approach in 2001. One of the goals behind the idea is to provide a Willow Creek experience within a thirty-minute drive of anyone in Chicagoland. The strategy is for each campus to be a fully functioning Willow Creek congregation. The preaching at each of the three current regional congregations is almost always presented via videocast as part of the design to provide the same teaching at each location. The other worship elements are usually live, and more live worship elements are added as local talent emerges. All programs, from children's ministry to adult small groups, are developed locally or are adapted from existing Willow Creek Community Church curricula to meet the needs of the local congregation.

An exciting two-way street of talent development is emerging between Willow Creek's regional campuses and the South Barrington campus. "Regional congregations provide people with serving and leadership opportunities they might never have at the South Barrington campus," explains Jim Tomberlin, formerly Willow Creek's regional pastor. "We're finding that opportunities and developing talent go both ways between the regionals and the South Barrington campus, giving leaders a chance to blossom."

> "We're finding that opportunities and developing talent go both ways between the regionals and the South Barrington campus."
> — Jim Tomberlin

9. Shift the ownership of programming to each local campus as much as possible. In most churches, it's hard to break into the existing leadership structures. New ministries often create a sense that there is a level playing field, making it easier for new talent to emerge and be accepted. So in almost every case when a church expands into multiple sites or venues, new players welcome the opportunities for significant ministry and leadership.

Willow Creek's regional congregations are an example of this principle. "The delivery of a videotape doesn't guarantee a successful church," says Jim Tomberlin. "It opens the door, it's the foundation, but you can't rely on a good video to guarantee a vibrant church service." The personality and distinctiveness of a regional campus needs to be highlighted and tailored into the programming. "Doing the programming ourselves builds more local ownership in each service," Jim says.

At Seacoast, we (Geoff) have given each of our campuses a great deal of leeway in the programming of weekend services. I quip that we frown on dancing girls and circus elephants for the most part, but beyond that, they have a lot of freedom to try new things. It's always fun to see how Seacoast finds expression in nine distinct communities and amazing to see the leadership that emerges.

The journey, however, has not been without pain. Our senior pastor, Greg Surratt says, "The bloodiest meeting I've ever been part of was when the staff told me that I was the problem, because everything triangulated through me," he says. "I've now learned to say, 'That sounds like a question for ___,' and I refer it to one of our campus pastors or to another staff member." Greg has done the same with much of the programming decision making.

The key to remaining one church while releasing the creative energy of our campuses is ensuring the transfer of DNA from the original campus to each new campus through the campus pastor. Each campus pastor comes "home" every other week to reconnect and maintains strong connections between meetings. Mac Lake, our leadership-development pastor, has the role of overseeing the campus pastors and ensuring the free flow of DNA.

10. Don't quit looking for a better way. What happens when a church pioneers something new and it works well? Other churches start asking its leaders for advice and insights. People make phone calls, send emails, and visit the campus to experience it for themselves and to ask questions. When this happens, the pioneer church often sponsors a conference, creates some resources, and posts a Frequently Asked Questions section on their website.

That's been the model for North Coast Church in Vista, California, the high-visibility pioneer of a video-venue approach to church expansion, with more than two-thirds of its 6,000 people choosing to worship each week at its video venues. Even though the North Coast team has been doing training conferences longer than most others, they make it very clear that they are still learning. "The video venue is a delivery system with a lot of unexplored opportunity," says Chris Mavity, who serves as executive director of the North Coast Training Network. "We are still exploring, trying to find new things that work, and work well." Chris's attitude and humility are typical of places that turn out top-notch leaders. They spot an opportunity, live in an ongoing quest to make the most of it, and train others while they themselves keep learning.

> "We are still exploring, trying to find new things that work, and work well."
> – Chris Mavity

How are superior leaders developed? According to Bobb Biehl (www.MasterPlanningGroup.com), author of numerous books on leadership and mentoring, "The most common answer I've heard from great leaders in Christendom is this: 'I took on things that were over my head and scrambled to find answers for them.'" There's a right way and a wrong way to handle that scramble. "Most churches don't have formal or consistent staff-development processes," explains Bobb. "Typically they give assignments and assume staff members know what they're doing. They think staff members are growing as leaders because the church or select ministries are growing."

One of the growth variables relates to timing. "Mentoring is not dumping all you know onto the protégé," Bobb says. "It's finding the teachable moment to ask, 'What are your plans?' and 'How can I help?'"

> "Most leaders grow on a need-to-know or need-to-grow basis."
> – Larry Osborne

Larry Osborne, lead pastor at North Coast, agrees. "Most leaders grow on a need-to-know

People-Development Strategies at Southwest Airlines

At Southwest Airlines, when they talk about developing leaders, they talk about "influencing people" through walking the talk, focusing on that which can be controlled, being prepared, showing how much you care, listening, and having open communication. Their leadership development program, housed in their unique University of People, is centered around these ten people strategies:

1. Attract and hire people who fit the culture
2. Let people be themselves
3. Create a learning community
4. Provide opportunity for growth and development
5. If they don't fit, say "goodbye"
6. You told me once, but tell me again
7. Avoid elitism and bureaucracy
8. Be flexible and do the right thing
9. Give awards and celebrate everything
10. Encourage people to act like owners[6]

or need-to-grow basis," he says. "Our video venues grow just like any other church. Unless you have a host pastor who understands leadership and group dynamics, the growth stops. If a ministry doesn't have strong leaders, it falters." In short, churches face a leader-making challenge because ministries cannot grow or stay healthy without leaders. Teachable reflection is one of the factors that leads to the formation of great leaders.

What's Your Leadership Incubator?

"Most of our pastors come from high-producing volunteers," says Greg Surratt, my older brother, "so we reward producers." In order to give maximum development and empowerment to everyone who volunteers, Seacoast has created a leadership pipeline (see illustration on p. 161), inspired by a book with that same title.[7]

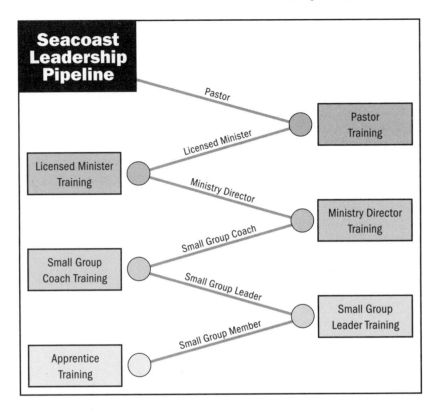

"Our vision at Seacoast is to reach unchurched people and lead them to become fully devoted followers of Christ," Greg says. "Everything we do is geared to that one goal. We need all the leaders we can raise up to help get us there."

With that attitude, Seacoast — and any other multi-site church — is very likely to find and empower all the leaders it needs. As Jesus reminded his followers, the ultimate answer to the leader-making challenge is a God who calls and sends: "The harvest is plentiful, but the workers are few. Ask the Lord of the harvest, therefore, to send out workers into his harvest field" (Luke 10:2).

One of our major challenges in writing this chapter was to keep it to a reasonable size. (At one point, we envisioned a three-volume set, but our publisher felt that was overkill.) Scores of excellent books, both secular and church related, have been written on leadership development, and many provide practical insight into the topic. Our intent has been to share insights from successful multi-site churches. As a practical resource, we reference several tools in the Multi-Site Toolbox in appendix A that will aid you in the leadership-development process. One helps you assess the qualities you will look for in your new leaders. Another helps your campus-pastor candidates identify their strengths and weaknesses and helps you build a development program customized for them.

When you finish with the leadership tools, turn to chapter 12, Leveraging Technology. Finally, we get to play with all the new, high-tech toys! Maybe.

Leveraging Technology

Find the right balance of technology, whether you use in-person teaching or video

> For some say, "His letters are weighty and forceful, but in person he is unimpressive and his speaking amounts to nothing." Such people should realize that what we are in our letters when we are absent, we will be in our actions when we are present."
> — 2 Corinthians 10:10-11

The idea of leveraging the latest technology for kingdom service is nothing new. Nor is the pushback, questioning, or occasional controversy raised by such changes. When I (Warren) was visiting relatives in Germany, I toured a famous medieval monastery in Germany. I learned how they took the church into the community by doing religious dramas. To reach the most people, they performed some of the dramas at night, which raised the need for lighting. By putting candles in front of colored glass, they created colored lighting, much like today's stage lights. "Was this controversial?" I asked our guide. "What do *you* think?" she responded with a smile.

Reading church history is fascinating because it reminds us that every generation asks about the appropriateness of using technology to do church. In America in the last two hundred years, these discussions have moved from "Should we pave over our gravel now that most people use cars rather than horses?" to "Should we replace the church outhouse with indoor plumbing?" to "Should we put a telephone in the church building?" to "Do we really need to use microphones?" to "If we put nighttime spotlights on our outdoor cross, will it draw people to put their hope in Christ?" to "How often should we update our church Internet site, since it forms a first impression for so many of our guests?"

All churches today, including multi-site churches, use technology in one way or another, from cell phones to email, from video cameras to special lighting. Is a specific and unique technology required for a church to become multi-site? No. In particular, does a church have to use videocasts to be multi-site? No. Will people have emotional reactions to the technological changes you make? Yes. Will some of those responses be strong? Perhaps.

Technology and Teaching

When my (Geoff's) pastor first suggested that we use videocast sermons at our church service, I thought it was the dumbest idea I had ever heard. I don't like to watch preachers on television, and I think talking heads on television news shows are mind-numbing, so why would anyone want to go sit in a school or a theater or even a church building and watch a preacher on a video screen?

So my pastor sent me on a field trip to experience video teaching at North Point, where Andy Stanley is pastor. On the drive to Atlanta, my mind went over all the reasons videocasts wouldn't work. (Why wait until after I'd experienced it to prepare my critique?)

Once there, I crossed my arms and hated it, as planned, until about five minutes into the sermon. "Wait a minute, what did he just say?" I asked myself as one of his insights connected with me. Soon I didn't really care, and almost forgot, that the sermon was on video. I was connecting to the content; the container didn't really matter.

I became a true believer that day in the leverage of using video to teach the good news. This has also been the reaction of thousands of people who have attended our video venues at Seacoast in the years since. People regularly comment to me, "We didn't think we would like the video, but after a few minutes, we didn't really notice that the sermon wasn't live."

The same is true in other churches where the technology has truly leveraged the impact on the congregation. An earlier example in this book described the pastor who raced from site to site in his car so that he could arrive just in time to preach; after his sermon, he would hop back in his car and race to the next campus. Another pastor, Craig Groeschel of Life Church in Oklahoma City, preaches the same number of times each weekend, but through videocast technology, he is able to cover more than twenty-five services each weekend in seven church locations across Oklahoma and Arizona. As one news service quipped about Life Church, "In the reality TV age, perhaps it's no surprise that fast-growth churches increasingly use cameras to put their pastors in two places—or three or four or more—at the same time."[1] If necessary, Craig could preach only once each weekend, and the multiplication effect would still work.

Pros and Cons of Video Teaching

This book offers specific examples from more than fifty multi-site churches, which are listed in appendix C. The first column of that list notes how the main teaching is delivered to the church's additional sites. Does it happen in person, with each site having its own preacher? Does the teaching come via videocast (whether live or prerecorded)? Or is it a combination of the two—video in some places, and in-person teaching in other campuses? Our list is almost evenly divided into thirds, as the diagram below illustrates.

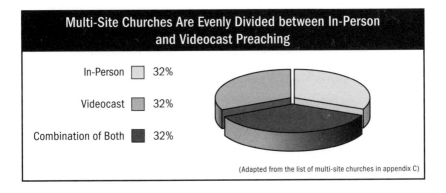

Multi-Site Churches Are Evenly Divided between In-Person and Videocast Preaching

In-Person ☐ 32%

Videocast ☐ 32%

Combination of Both ■ 32%

(Adapted from the list of multi-site churches in appendix C)

The fairly equal distribution shows that churches are able to make all of these approaches work. Here are some general observations drawn from what we've heard and experienced at churches that do some or all their teaching by video.

Biggest Pros

1. It focuses attention on making the sermon and delivery the best possible. The awareness that more than one congregation or site will experience the sermon inspires those involved in the production of the service to put extra attention into everything from sermon preparation to sound quality to stage design.

2. It gives a church the opportunity to extend its ministry to new places with a consistency of values, akin to the trusted-name feel associated with the opening of a new Starbucks or Krispy Kreme location.

3. It invites new talent to emerge and develop, both musicians and campus pastors, at size-appropriate settings. Many campus pastors and musicians have started in small video cafés, where they gained the skill and confidence to enable them to meet the expectations of a larger or higher-risk venue.

Biggest Cons

1. Technological failures could disrupt the environment of worship and spiritual mentoring.

2. Preachers can unintentionally speak in ways that are distracting or confusing to listeners at other sites.

3. Other aspiring teachers don't have as many opportunities to develop their gifts since using videocasts decreases the number of people who preach each week.

Live versus a One-Week Video Delay

Some churches, such as Northland – A Church Distributed, in Longwood, Florida, use live videocasts, and some even link their campuses in seamless two-way worship, as described in "On a Mission from God" (chapter 4). Northland's heart is for people to have the heavenly experience of sensing "a great multitude that no one could count, from every nation, tribe, people, and language" (Rev. 7:9). Northland wants its sites to have this sense of connection whenever it is technologically possible to do so.

Other churches, such as the various campuses of North Point, based in metropolitan Atlanta, Georgia, likewise try to emulate what's happening in a live auditorium, but they do so with a one-week delay. For its Buckhead campus, North Point uses three screens. Two screens on the sides offer image magnification of the band and the preacher, song lyrics, a sermon outline, and support messages. A large wide-format center screen, measuring eighteen feet by twenty-two feet, runs from the ceiling to the floor. The camera never pans or zooms. The high-definition playback (currently using a Christie Digital Systems Roadster S9 with rear projection and a surround-sound speaker system) is remarkably lifelike, having a three-dimensional effect almost like a hologram. People seated behind the first few rows "occasionally look to the center, but mainly watch the image magnification," says David McDaniel, who has been in a leadership role since Buckhead's 2001 launch.

Why a one-week delay? "We're chicken!" David says. He appreciates the seven days of padding that allows any technical glitches to be solved and allows the staff to refine the programming to support the videocast. Only Easter and Christmas need to be specially recorded; otherwise the one-week delay doesn't present a problem because the sermons don't tie into themes like Mother's Day or put specific dates on events ("this afternoon's Super Bowl game").

Tips for Making Engaging Videocast Sermons

1. At or near the beginning of each message, look directly at a camera.

2. Likewise, at drive-it-home moments, eyeball the camera.

3. Verbally mention the off-site during the sermon so that they'll feel included.

4. Avoid shots that remind video viewers that they're *not* there.

5. Make sure the videocast includes anything the speaker references.

What If We Can't Afford to Use Video?

If your church already uses image magnification in its services or has a television broadcast, making the move to videocast messages is fairly simple. For many churches, however, moving into the realm of video can be daunting. The answer to the question, "How much will video cost?" is often, "How much are you willing to pay?" Video doesn't have to break the bank, however.

Let's look at how your church can begin using videocast sermons without breaking the bank. Starting from scratch, a church can be up and running with good-quality video at an off-site campus for around $10,000.

First you'll need a video camera. You can spend tens of thousands of dollars on a broadcast-quality camera, but it isn't necessary in many situations. A suitable camera for most churches can cost less than $3,000 (currently the Canon GL2 is popular in churches). Be sure to invest in a professional tripod and theatrical lighting for the speaker. Creating an interesting backdrop for the speaker and making sure it is well-lit is also helpful.

Although churches often use four or more cameras for television broadcasts, it is possible to provide a good experience for viewers at a second campus using just one camera. (Remember that if the speaker were live, the audience would only have one "camera" angle—their own.) One camera works best when the speaker is somewhat station-ary; you will need an experienced operator to follow a moving target. Position the camera at eye level with the speaker. Frame the shot from about waist up. (If you use a wider shot, you'll need a higher-end cam-era and projector to get a clear picture.) The closer you are able to position the camera to the speaker, the smoother the picture will be when you pan the camera. Adding a second camera will give a great deal of flexibility in adding wider shots or covering the action when there is more than one speaker, but a second camera also adds a great deal of expense.

For playback at the campus, you'll probably do best with a mini DV player, a video projector, and a screen. You can pay $20,000 or more just for a video projector, but in many cases a relatively inexpensive projector is all you need.

Obviously, as you add bells and whistles, the price for video will continue to climb, but you can get started very economically and see great results. When we (Geoff) started off-site campuses at Seacoast, we would record our message on several S-VHS tape recorders hooked together. As soon as the service was over, the local campus pastors would drop by the video room and pick up their tapes for the next day. I would grab the tapes for the distant campuses and rush them to the Greyhound bus station, where I would put the tapes on the next bus out of town. Our motto at that time was "We'll go anywhere Greyhound goes." We've gotten a little more sophisticated now (we pay someone to take the tapes to the bus), but we have seen God use video to reach thousands of people without spending a great deal of money. That's why we call it "leveraging" technology.

What's Your Next Step?

When it comes to technology and multi-size churches, one size doesn't fit all. Many churches successfully use live teaching at all of their sites, some use a mixture of video and in-person, and some have live simulcasts involving several campuses. Notice the variety of approaches in the chart on the following pages.

Finding the right technology for your church will be driven by vision, values, and budget, but the right decisions can help open the door to God's next step for the ministry of your church. The wrong decision can lead to detours. We'll help you avoid some of those detours in the next chapter.

Quick Facts: Multi-Site Technology

An Overview of Five Different Approaches Used by Multi-Site Locations

Church name	Bethlehem Baptist Church	Fellowship Bible Church	The Garden at St. Luke's	Northland—A Church Distributed	Seacoast Church
Campus name	Bethlehem North Campus	Fellowship Bible South	The Mansion at Oak Hill	Northland at Mount Dora	Seacoast Church—Irmo
Campus location	Mounds View, MN	Benton, AR	Carmel, IN	Mount Dora, FL	Irmo, SC
Distance	13 miles	18 miles	12 miles	28 miles	125 miles
Site number	Second	Second	Third	Third	Fourth
How do you get video to the site?	Hand-delivered tape	Hand-delivered disc	T-1 line	6 T-1 lines	Download it, then burn DVD
What type of media is it?	DvdPro tape	DVD	Live feed	Live feed	DVD
If recorded, how long ago?	Same weekend (Saturday night service, played on Sunday)	One week delay	n/a	n/a	Same weekend (Saturday night service, played on Sunday)
If recorded, how is it edited?	No edits	Edited after it's recorded	n/a	n/a	Edited after it's recorded
How many cameras are involved?	1 (straight-on front shot); the church has 3 cameras but found that switching angles during the message reinforces the sense of watching a "production."	2 (mostly head-on).	1 (simple head shot); the church has 2 cameras available at each site and uses them for other parts of the service.	4 at Dog Track Road campus (the original campus), 2 at Mount Dora site, (plus 3 at Lyman site, and 3 at West Oaks site).	2 (mostly head-on).

What's the backup plan if you lose the signal or the equipment fails?	Two formats are recorded at the Saturday night service: one DvdPro tape and one DVD backup.	None!	1. An earlier service is recorded on DVD, which could be driven to Oak Hill if a problem arises. 2. If this fails, one of the pastors at Oak Hill would read the message to the congregation.	1. We have a 300K Windows Media stream that comes on separate DSL line. 2. The Saturday night service is recorded on DVD. Both backups lose the two-way dynamic.	1. The campus pastor would preach live from sermon notes. 2. A backup copy would be played from the hard drive of a laptop. 3. We have an "emergency kit" containing VHS tapes of old messages.
Do you use additional projection during the videocast?	Only text for worship lyrics	Image magnification with PowerPoint graphics included	Scriptures or quotes are superimposed, keeping speaker's voice but substituting words on screen	2 DL–1's at Dog Track Road campus for art or graphics, plus occasional projection or plasma screens for virtual people placement at all campuses	Nothing added to support the videocast
How many people on tech team at this off-site?	Minimum of 3	1	3	1, plus occasional volunteer	5
What are the main tech roles at this off-site?	1 sound person, 1 video person (plays back video, runs cameras for image magnification, switches video mixer during service), 1 PowerPoint/lights person	1 person to press "play" and "stop" on DVD player at appropriate times	1 sound and lighting person; 2 people to coordinate slides, video, the mixer, and communication with Oak Hill via cell phone	Primarily mix audio, run light cues, and position movement of robotic camera, 1 person	1 sound person, 1 lighting technician, 1 set designer, 1 computer and DVD operator, and 1 service producer/technical director

Church name	Bethlehem Baptist Church	Fellowship Bible Church	The Garden at St. Luke's	Northland—A Church Distributed	Seacoast Church
Which tech staff, if any, are paid?	None now, but in the future each campus will have one paid full-time or part-time person.	No one (all volunteer).	The sound and lighting person is paid.	The main person is paid.	No one (all volunteer).
Site worship attendance	1,200 (across two services)	500 (across two services)	200 (one service)	200 (one service)	475 (across two services)
What's the next-step technology dream at your site?	In the near future, the Mounds View site will have its own DvdPro deck. Currently one deck is shuttled between campuses. Having a second deck will allow each site to record high-quality video independently.	We are looking for live delivery solutions.	After upgrading the mixing and switching equipment, the next step is to expand the size of the connection between sites to improve the quality of the images, which probably means more T-1 lines.	We are testing a 5.8Ghz wireless link at the church's fourth site to allow 50MB/sec data throughput. If it succeeds in eliminating encoding or transmission delays, church may use it for this site too.	We want faster downloads with fewer skips.
Location of original campus	Minneapolis, MN	Little Rock, AR	Indianapolis, IN	Longwood, FL	Mount Pleasant, SC
Denomination	Baptist General Conference	Nondenominational	United Methodist	Nondenominational	Nondenominational
Church age	134 years	28 years	52 years	40 years	17 years
Year you became multi-site	2002	2004	1995	2001	2002
Internet address	www.bbcmpls.org	www.fbclr.org	www.the-garden.org	www.northlandcc.org	www.seacoast.org

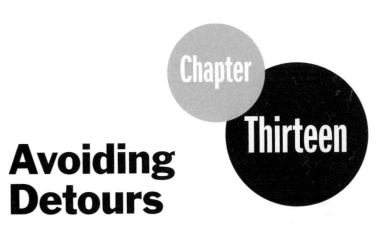

Avoiding Detours

Learn important lessons from churches that have taken wrong turns or hit roadblocks

> The wisdom of the wise keeps life on track; the foolishness of fools lands them in the ditch. — Proverbs 14:8 MESSAGE

A year into Seacoast's multi-site journey, a bright young man who was new to Seacoast approached us (Geoff) about the possibility of starting a campus in his hometown of Portland, Oregon. "Seacoast Portland"—what a great idea! We had never been to Portland, but it sounded nice. We had already opened four campuses, how hard could one more be? We enrolled Brad into our started-because-of-him campus-pastor training program, and after three months of intense wedding planning (he was getting married and starting a church at the same time), we sent him off, underresourced and overconfident, to open Seacoast Portland.

Who knew that Portland is seventy miles from the nearest seacoast (sand) and three thousand miles from the nearest Seacoast (church)? Brad did his best, but after six months, we all decided that Seacoast Portland wasn't going to fly (or run, or walk, or crawl for that matter).

Brad now has a successful ministry, a great marriage, and a good story to tell his grandkids about a crazy church in South Carolina. Seacoast is better for the experience, having learned to go into only communities we understand and to send only leaders we know well. Hopefully these lessons will keep us and others from wandering down the same dead ends.

Ten Detours to Avoid

The following insights come from churches that have developed a healthy multiple-location approach to ministry. The insights are largely answers to these questions: "What is your best piece of wisdom for other churches, based on what you experienced?" and "How can you save them pain or accelerate their progress?"

In that spirit, here is what various multi-site pioneers said they wish they had known before they started.

1. Remember that multi-site isn't a vision by itself, but a vehicle to achieve the vision. Generally, the multi-site approach is used to solve a problem, such as running out of room, or to take advantage of a new opportunity. At North Coast Church in Vista, California, worshipers can currently choose between five locations, five worship times, and six worship styles. That adds up to more than twenty options or services a weekend! Yet pastor Larry Osborne has consistently found that "video venues are a great ministry tool but a pathetic engine."

2. As you look for staff, remember that multi-site leaders need strong relational skills. Chartwell Baptist Church, in a suburb of Toronto, Ontario, has been multi-site since 1993. It has campuses in four locations. "More than anything, we've learned the absolute importance of making sure any staff you hire are highly relational," says Peter Roebbelen, team leader of the pastoral staff. "At first we hired for expertise, which seems great on paper, but people without relational sensitivities don't work well in the complex matrix environment of a multi-site church."

> "More than anything, we've learned the absolute importance of making sure any staff you hire are highly relational."
> – Peter Roebbelen

3. Make sure each site has a "face with the place"—a campus pastor or venue director. "We underestimated the role of campus pastor as leader, at first looking primarily for an emcee," says Kevin Penry, a pastor and operational leader at Life Church in Oklahoma City. "This person needs to be someone that others are willing to follow." The church has five campuses in Oklahoma and two in Arizona, plus an online campus, all of which bring the sermon by video from the North Oklahoma City or Edmond campus. This structure causes the campus pastors at Life Church to need not only relationship skills for leading a campus but also the ability to convey equity to the screen. "A campus pastor has got to believe in our approach to such an extent that he imparts credibility to the screen," says Kevin.

4. *When experimenting, try a low-regret, high-return strategy.* Restated: look for what you can do with minimum regret and maximum impact.

When Seacoast started the Annex, which was our first foray into the world of multi-site, we wanted to wow the masses, so we pulled out all the stops (for us anyway). In a space that comfortably seats 300, we installed a sound system that could adequately handle the Rolling Stones at Madison Square Garden. A consultant recommended we install a 6' by 9' video screen, so we balked and found one that was twelve feet high and seventeen feet wide. (People in the front row were often frightened by our pastor's giant head on the screen.) We installed nine television monitors, enough equipment to open our own Starbucks, and a trendy loft to ensure the "cool" factor. All this in a facility we were leasing in a retail center just under a mile from our original campus. While the Annex has been a success, we have subsequently discovered that we don't need all the bells and whistles.

Likewise, Stillwater United Methodist Church in Dayton, Ohio, spent $1.2 million to relocate the original church but only $50,000 to launch its second site in Englewood, according to Duane Anders, lead pastor at the Stillwater site. Ongoing costs have also been proportionally smaller at the second site.

5. *Avoid adopting a mature organizational structure when you're smaller.* Fellowship Bible Church in Little Rock, Arkansas, offers three on-campus worship venues, each a different size. Tim Lundy, the directional leader and a teaching pastor, compares the need for greeters at a small drugstore to that of Wal-Mart: At the mom-and-pop store it happens automatically, but Wal-Mart intentionally positions greeters

as you enter and has a rule for employees that if someone gets within ten feet, the employee is to greet them. "The bigger you are, the more directional you need to be about how to be a welcoming church," he says. "In smaller site locations, you can rely on natural relationships to make things work, but in larger venues you need more global rules."

6. *Don't view multi-site as merely an add-on, since being part of a multi-site church will change who you are.* Either multi-site will change you, or you'll have a stepchild who will languish or leave you. Craig Cheney, the worship-venue overseer at Fellowship Bible Church in Little Rock, says, "Multi-site is a culture shift, not a tactical addition. When we went multi-site, we became a fundamentally different church. Multi-site has not only changed our perspective but our practices of church as well." There is a big difference between being a church with multiple sites and being a multiple-site church.

7. *Whatever small groups did for you as a single campus still needs to happen at each new site.* In most multiple-location churches, small groups play a vital role. Group life serves as each site's relational glue, the muscle for doing ministry, and a primary context for leadership development. Jacksonville Chapel in Lincoln Park, New Jersey, is diligent about guarding its small groups. "That is our DNA," says Warren Hunt, worship pastor. "Small groups are a driving force for disciple-making as they focus on welcome, worship, Word, and world."

The small groups emphasis can also be anything but a detour; it can be a viable way to form new campuses. For example, Dave Browning in Mount Vernon, Washington, says, "The engine of Christ the King is small groups. Our vision is a church that will convene in hundreds of small groups, with worship centers strategically located in every community. The decentralization of our worship centers naturally follows the decentralized approach we have already taken with small groups. When we look to enter a new community, we first try to develop at least two small groups in that community. Then, when the time is right, we begin a café, as a 'convention of cells.' If the small group is truly where a person's needs for caring and community are met, then the location and size of the worship center is a secondary consideration, provided that meaningful worship and teaching are present."

8. *Avoid the term "main campus" because it implies that the other sites are second class.* Many churches begin identifying their campuses

by geography, such as Willow Creek South Barrington, Willow Creek North Shore, Willow Creek McHenry County, and Willow Creek Wheaton. Christ the King Church in Mount Vernon, Washington, does likewise with its many locations, calling Mount Vernon the original campus when necessary. To prevent the sense that everything is better at the mother church, churches like Christ the King have actually moved central support—accounting, churchwide graphics, marketing, and office support—out of the original campus. "I wish we had figured out sooner that our centralized support services need to be separate from the worship center," says founding Pastor Dave Browning. "We use the term 'worship center' instead of 'main campus' so that every center is on equal par."

9. *Learn the difference between replicating a site and replicating impact.* Dave Browning at Christ the King Church is developing simple and fast ways to add a large number of new sites in any given year. "We want to multiply impact, not just sites," he says. "With each new site, we want people to sense that something is going on that's way bigger than us." For Dave, people at each new site need to be driven by the sake of the mission, not by the convenience of having a shorter drive time. Otherwise, the potential spiritual impact is diminished.

10. *Don't underestimate the many contexts in which a multi-site approach can significantly help fulfill your church's mission.* Chris Mavity, executive director of North Coast Training Network, has launched successful video venues in everything from warehouses to public schools to a drug-and-alcohol rehabilitation center. "I am continually surprised by the types of worship service locations [potential host sites] who are interested in multi-site," he says, referring to many untapped niche locations his church would like to explore.

Jim Tomberlin, regional pastor for Willow Creek until 2005, sees the extension possibilities of multi-site. According to Jim, "In the future, multi-site will be a primary church-planting tool. Multi-site is also the logical and inevitable next step of a megachurch. If a church is so well endowed with gifting and anointing, it would be tragic to keep it in one container. Multi-site multiplies ministry exponentially because it maximizes seats at optimal attendance hours, and its return on investment in money and people is far greater."

Greg Surratt, pastor of Seacoast Church (did I mention he's my *older* brother?), sees multi-site taking churches to places they've not previously been able to go. "Multi-site may be the only vehicle big enough to complete the Great Commission," he says.

Churches That Try, "Fail," and Are Better for It

The following stories represent churches that went the multi-site direction but didn't end up staying there, at least, not for now. None consider the experience a failure. All found value in it, and each matured in the process. Here are the benefits they gained.

1. Learning to keep priority on leadership development. New Life Christian Fellowship in Chesapeake, Virginia, was facing a problem of trying to fit too much growth within too little property. One day as the senior pastor, Bobby Hill, was reflecting on the "all you need is empty vessels" message of 2 Kings 4:1–7, he had a vision of a multiplying church. As New Life would make space, God would be faithful to fill it. New Life would become one church in many locations as a multi-congregational church.

New Life launched its first off-site expansion in 1996, commissioning 200 of its 650 regular attendees to a new site about six miles away. A second satellite congregation was birthed just over a year later. Motivated primarily by evangelistic outreach, New Life continued to multiply congregations, with a total of six in the Chesapeake area by 2000.

Bobby Hill resigned in 2001, and the new senior director, Joseph Umidi, modified the vision to become that of an autonomous but connected family of churches. "Within ten years, we hope to have at least a dozen congregations in the area," Joseph says. Bobby Hill now serves as director of Vanguard Ministries, an apostolic network of leaders and church-planting churches.

Why didn't New Life continue as one church in many locations? The biggest stretch was the need for New Life to increase its pipeline of volunteers and new leaders. For its first off-site, New Life sent out some of its most experienced people. Then New Life recruited new people, trained them, and sent some of them to the next new site. As former staff pastor Jerry Graham points out, "The multi-site model requires significantly more lay leaders" than most other approaches, so New

Life "had to purposefully raise up an unusual number of leaders."[1] Joseph adds, "We didn't have the caliber of leaders that could leave their legacy by training others."

Are there regrets about the transition? "All of us would rather have stayed with multi-site," Joseph says. Are there regrets that the church *started* as a multi-site? None. "There was a lot of excitement during Bobby's time, which has helped motivate us to do the hard work of mentoring, training, and developing more leaders."

In short, multi-site didn't work long-term for this church because it couldn't develop enough leaders to keep up with all the opportunities associated with rapid expansion into multiple sites. But the leader-making challenge has been a welcome one, both then and now. As New Life discovered, leadership development is the number one essential for building and maintaining a multi-site church. (See "Building Better Leaders," chapter 11, for ways other churches have solved the leadership-development challenge, and appendix A for tools that can be used in leadership development for multi-site churches.)

2. Modeling a way to give unselfishly. Ginghamsburg Church, a United Methodist congregation in Tipp City, Ohio, runs eight weekly worship services on its primary campus. "It's a stewardship issue," says Mike Slaughter, lead pastor. "We want to reuse our facilities as much as possible."

Mike had the same attitude when he was contacted by his bishop, who was planning to close Medway United Methodist Church, an aging, dying congregation twenty miles away. He asked Ginghamsburg to take it under its wing and give it one last shot to redevelop it. "We did a mock-up with our logo and Medway's, calling it 'one church with the same DNA,'" Mike says. "We sent a team of our people there, and I mentored one of them to become the pastor."

The redevelopment has gone extremely well. Within eighteen months, attendance was climbing through 150, with many conversions reported. The average age of attendees has dropped thirty years, and the handful of children that attended the church has grown to fifty during that same period.

During two years of mentoring and support, all the while being infused with Ginghamsburg's DNA, Medway has shifted from life-support status to being an official extension of Ginghamsburg to now being on its own, with the layperson Ginghamsburg sent appointed as its full-time pastor.[2]

"It is now a self-sustaining church, though still in full dependence on the Holy Spirit," Mike says. "They have our DNA, and they might have become our ninth worship site. But they regained their identity so fast that they didn't need my name or the Ginghamsburg name."

Medway is again on its own two feet, and Ginghamsburg is looking out for other opportunities to use a multi-site approach, if applicable.

3. Using multiple sites to gain a better foothold. The Journey, a young church that meets on the island of Manhattan in New York City, held its first worship service on Easter 2002. "When we started, we couldn't decide between the Upper West Side and Greenwich Village downtown," says Nelson Searcy, lead pastor. So the church went to both. From its opening day, The Journey was one church in two locations. "Neither site was large enough to stand on its own, but together we had enough strength in numbers to keep moving forward," explains Nelson."

In 2005, the church was able to rent a very large, well-located ballroom for worship services, so it consolidated in one location but offered three service times, and ultimately four. "I wasn't happy about going to one location," says Nelson. "I looked forward to doing multi-site again, because we can reach more people and offer more options that way."

In early 2006, the church went back to two locations. "My dream down the road is to be in all the professional sections of New York City's five boroughs," Nelson says.

Are You Still a Learner?

As we reflect on different multi-site church leaders that we've known and watched, we'd love to say that they take fewer missteps, on average, than other pastors. But that wouldn't be true. If anything, they tend to be risk takers. They'd rather try something on faith than sit still and do nothing.

Our sense is that faith, by definition, contains an element of risk. As Michael Slaughter writes in *UnLearning Church*:

> The disciples, riding in a small boat battling fierce waves and winds, see Jesus walking calmly across the water. They are all terrified.

In all their panic of going against the wind, the disciples forgot that Jesus would not be distant and uninvolved. Jesus was right there with them, walking on the water. Yet most of them couldn't recognize him. They thought he was a ghost.

Peter, on the other hand, gets out of the boat and walks on the water because his faith tells him that it's really Jesus out there. When he notices the strong wind, he becomes frightened. Beginning to sink, he cries out, "Lord, save me!" Jesus immediately reaches out his hand and catches him, saying, "You of little faith, why did you doubt?" (Matthew 14:30–31 [NRSV]).

Peter is the only one who risked. He chose to block out the voice of the storm. Instead, he focused on Jesus who said, "Come." Peter did the impossible because he responded to the voice of Jesus instead of listening to the storms of life and fears of others.

Peter didn't begin to experience problems until he began to pay attention to the raging water through his physical eyes. He got in trouble when he began to look at the raging storm rather than look into the eyes of the one who had said, "Follow me" (Matthew 4:19).[3]

As you think about using a multi-site approach to reach people for Jesus, don't be fearful of potential detours. Instead, step out of the boat and keep your eyes on Jesus—and you'll be in good company.

why extend further *and* reach more people?

Secrets of Ongoing Replication

Don't let your dream stop short of developing an entire movement of replicating campuses

> Then the church throughout Judea, Galilee and Samaria enjoyed a time of peace. It was strengthened; and encouraged by the Holy Spirit, it grew in numbers, living in the fear of the Lord. — Acts 9:31

In the next few days, take a look around at how many Harley-Davidson bikers you see—how they dress, what age they are, and what gender. How has Harley, named Forbes 2001 Company of the Year, replicated the biker movement, raising up a new-generation "cult" of leather and do-rag-wearing fans? Several years ago, a team from Leadership Network took one hundred church leaders to the Kansas City plant that assembles many of the Harley motorcycles. The goal was to get answers to how Harley built a movement and then did it again.

For Harley, the key was their understanding that movements are all about people and, in their case, reaching *new* groups of riders. As

James Ziemer, chief financial officer of Harley-Davidson, Inc., said, "We don't need new customers today; we don't need them tomorrow. But we may ten years from now." The company realized the age of their customer base was increasing every year and also that they were reaching only a small segment of females. Their corporate growth could not be sustained through those demographics.

Harley began by asking the question, "What barriers of entry are keeping a new group of riders from buying motorcycles, and how could the barriers be turned into opportunities?" Harley's answer was that new groups did not know how to ride, so it hired younger leaders to design and implement a training program called "the Rider's Edge." Harley created an experience that helped new riders not only learn the basics of riding but also get to know the dealer and mechanics, as well as the lifestyle of motorcycling.

Churches wanting to replicate campuses might ask the same question: "What are the barriers, and how can they be turned into opportunities?" This chapter will introduce you to the barriers associated with adding a second or third campus and with the additional complexity of moving to eight, ten, or more locations. It will provide you with secrets of success that will help you turn barriers into opportunities for developing experiences that lead to an entire movement of replicating campuses.

How Transferable Is Your Weekend Service?

One of the first challenges we (Geoff) had to face at Seacoast when we ventured outside our little beach community was that our weekend services were often peppered with references and stories that made sense only in Mount Pleasant, South Carolina. Our pastor would talk about going over the old bridge, visiting Town Center, and spending time on IOP (the Isle of Palms). All the locals understood exactly what he was talking about, but people watching the sermon one hundred miles away were completely lost. "Driving down Johnnie Dodds" takes on a whole new meaning for people who don't know that Johnnie Dodds Boulevard is the main street in our town. We realized we either had to explain local references or find more universal illustrations to connect with a wider audience.

How transferable are *your* weekend services? Can someone who has never been to your town, has never heard of your church, and has no background with your traditions understand what happens during a service? This weekend watch and listen to what is communicated during your service as though you were a complete stranger. Listen for code words that need explanations, references to specific people in the congregation, and remarks about local locations.

Here is an example of what a pastor might say in a message, with trouble spots highlighted: "Good morning. [What if it's evening when this message is seen?] Isn't this a beautiful day? [It may be pouring down rain where the congregation is]. I hope you enjoyed that great song by Sue today. [If the music is not on video, they won't know who Sue is or what song she sang.] If you're new today, be sure to join me after the service in the fellowship hall for the newcomers' reception. [If the congregation is forty miles away, how will they join you? And where is the fellowship hall?] As we get started, take a look at the video screen. [People at other sites are already looking at the video screen.]"

> The more you can change and adapt your local mannerisms, the easier it will be to replicate your church in new communities.

Other regional factors to look at are the style and context of your services. If your messages are focused on reaching a narrow demographic in your region, how transferable is the ministry? What about your style of worship? A style that appeals to baby boomers may not play well in a senior center or in a college town.

The key is to look at the content, style, and context of your weekend services with fresh eyes. When you discover things that may not transfer well to other campuses or other regions, you then need to ask, "Are these things we can change or adapt, or are these nonnegotiable?" The more you can change and adapt your local mannerisms, the easier it will be to replicate your church in new communities.

What Are Your Core Ministries?

Once you determine that your weekend service is transferable, the next question is, "What are the essential ministries that must be reproduced at every campus?" As a church grows over the years, it normally adds a variety of need-based ministries. Some churches can name over one hundred individual ministries at their original campus. Which of these are essential to the life and health of every campus? The longer the list of core ministries, the more difficult it will be to replicate.

A couple of years ago, I (Geoff) was talking with leaders at several churches that were all beginning to open multiple campuses. One leader said they had defined twelve core ministries they would reproduce at every campus. A second leader said they had reduced their core down to eight essential ministries. I felt a little embarrassed to say that at Seacoast we had identified four core areas we felt were crucial. Dave Browning of Christ the King in Washington trumped us all when he shared that they had only two indispensable ministries: worship and small groups. The issue for Christ the King is their ability to reach unchurched people through their worship services and to disciple them through small groups. While this approach may be too lean for most churches, it enabled Christ the King to open twelve campuses in six years.

> There is no right answer to the number of core ministries a church should have.

There is no right answer to the number of core ministries a church should have. Each church must understand its unique DNA and its mission from God. As you seek to replicate your DNA in one or more locations, be aware that a low number of core ministries that have to be reproduced will ease the process of replication.

Are Your Core Ministries Reproducible?

Once you have developed your list of essential ministries, the next task is to determine how reproducible they are. Often a growing church will put a lot of energy and resources into vital areas, such as the children's ministry. Ministry leaders may build elaborate sets, install expensive sound, video, and lighting systems, and create programming that requires highly talented and committed leaders. The challenge comes in trying to replicate this level of excellence several times in a variety of settings. Can the sets be reproduced and made portable? Can you afford high-end sound, video, and lighting systems at every site? Will you be able to find the tal-

> Before opening two, three, or more campuses, a great deal of thought and prayer must go into making core ministries replicable and scalable.

ented volunteers needed? Before opening two, three, or more campuses, a great deal of thought and prayer must go into making core ministries replicable and scalable.

Life Church has developed a number of ways to replicate itself. First, it found a unique answer for reproducing the amazing backdrops used at their initial campus. Artists in the church took digital photographs of all their sets and then turned each photograph into a vector drawing. Those drawings were then turned into wall-size replicas of the original sets by a company that prints vinyl billboards. Now every weekend at each of Life Church's temporary locations, the large, wall-size pictures are hung from the ceiling. At the end of the service, they are rolled up and stored. Second, to handle the sound and video needs of the children's ministry, planners created self-contained, rolling boxes with the sound system, projector, and DVD player inside. All the workers need to do each weekend is roll out the cart and plug it in. Finally, to ease the burden of finding enough talented teachers, Life Church produces its children's lessons on video and distributes them to each of its campuses.

Likewise, everything we do at Seacoast is evaluated in light of how it would work on fifteen or twenty campuses. (We have always adhered to the rabbit model of reproduction: if one off-site campus would be good, dozens would be great.) If a new ministry or program isn't going to be viable across the board, it probably isn't going to happen. (I recently proposed that all Seacoast pastors should be given Porsches to create a new sense of the Seacoast "brand." This didn't pass the viability test, but I'm still trying.)

> "Intentional leadership development must be there; otherwise, nothing else works."
> — Peter Roebbelen

Another aspect of reproducing ministries is finding and training the leaders necessary to operate those ministries. In a multiple-campus environment, leadership development quickly becomes the biggest challenge in reproduction. As Peter Roebbelen has learned at Chartwell Baptist Church, which has been multi-site since 1993, "Intentional leadership development must be there; otherwise, nothing else works." A rapidly reproducing church needs to develop talent farms for campus pastors, worship leaders, children's ministry directors, and any of its other core ministries.

Community Christian Church in Chicago has created a School for the Arts, in part to develop artists for their future campuses. According to arts director Eric Bramlett, "Our desire is to reproduce and develop leaders in all areas of the arts. We offer classes in visual art, vocal and instrumental music, rock music, video production, theater, dance, and more. We hire professional artists to develop curriculum and teach in our classes. Our goal as a school is to build up existing Community Christian artists into leaders, train Community Christian attendees who have a passion for the arts and want to contribute, and be a bridge to our surrounding community through arts education." The school, which has over four hundred students at five campuses, has been a great resource for the church.

What Is Your Financial and Administrative Plan for Reproduction?

One of the secrets of replication is to solve the administrative puzzle presented by multiple campuses. Decisions that are fairly straightforward in a single-site environment can quickly become complex when multiple campuses are spread across a wide region. For example, Seacoast currently leases ten different facilities in eight cities across two states. We are involved in four building projects, whose costs range from a few thousand to several million dollars. Our information-technology department supports eight different offices with a dizzying variety of equipment. (Our campus pastor in Greenville can't imagine being forced to use something besides his Macintosh computer, but everyone else is on a PC.) When a church adds two or more campuses, several key administrative questions must be answered:

1. *Where will financial decisions be made?* What financial decisions can be made at the campus level, and what will be handled centrally?
2. *How will multiple campuses be handled by the existing information-technology structure?* Will everyone be on the same network? Can your church database handle multiple locations? Several church software companies are currently developing database applications to address the unique challenges of multi-site churches. (These companies can be identified by asking around or by following magazines like *Christian Computing*, www.ccmag.com.)

3. *How much money are you willing to invest in each location?* Beyond the start-up budget, how much money can you put into the operating costs of a campus? Is there a point at which you will shut down a campus if it continues to be a drain on the budget?

4. *How will you stay connected to a large number of campuses?* As Seacoast has continued to expand, we have found the need to break our campuses down into bite-size chunks. (I'm speaking metaphorically; we've never actually eaten a campus.) One way we have accomplished this is by assigning our campuses to regions, which we began when we had seven campuses. In each region, we have asked one of our campus pastors to take on the additional role of regional coach. In addition to meetings with all the campus pastors, the regions meet together monthly for accountability, ideas, and support.

How Will You Safeguard the "Brand"?

Quality control is a major challenge when a church looks toward sponsoring three, five, or ten campuses. A copy of a copy of a copy does not always resemble the original. How can you ensure that the campuses will remain faithful to the vision and values of the original campus?

One of the best ways to do this is to make sure leaders know and understand the nonnegotiables of the DNA of the overall church. As we discussed in "Hitting the Sweet Spot" (chapter 9), the longer the list, the harder it will be to maintain at outlying campuses, but it's important that everyone know what level of variation is acceptable from campus to campus.

> A copy of a copy of a copy does not always resemble the original.

Another way to ensure that campuses remain faithful to your church's vision and values is to have at least one staff member who regularly visits all the campuses. It is helpful if the staff member has a checklist of items to look for in "quality checking" the sites to help them stay aligned with the overall vision (see appendix A for a link to the checklist Seacoast uses). It is also helpful for the senior pastor to visit the campuses often. Having the "big kahuna" on-site is a huge morale boost for the campuses. This gives the pastor a chance to see what is happening outside of the original location. It also helps reconnect the campus to the pastor's vision.

How Will You Continue to Reproduce?

Adding a second campus for many churches is a fairly straightforward proposition: find a site, train a leader, start a campus. The challenge is to keep the momentum going. If each campus is as hard to start as the previous campus, staff will begin to revolt at the thought of opening another site.

To be successful at ongoing replication, a multi-site church is like a car: it needs an engine, a transmission, and an owner's manual. The engine is the impetus for starting the next sight. It begins with a vision—a dream to reach people in a new community, to free up some seats in a full auditorium, or to reach another culture. You put the engine in gear by developing the right leaders, whether for your second campus or your tenth. As Dave Ferguson says, in reflecting back on the early days of Community Christian Church in Chicago, where he is founding pastor, "As we developed leaders, we took the step of adding a second service. We didn't wait to do that until we ran out of space or seats. Instead, we believed that if we had the leaders, God would send the people. So we added a second service within six months of starting Community Christian Church."[1] Today, Community Christian has more than twenty weekly celebration services on eight different campuses.

What then keeps the engine running? What keeps the vision alive? What keeps the staff from becoming fatigued? At Seacoast, we (Geoff) have built the idea of replication into each campus from the beginning. Each of our campuses is expected to replicate itself as soon as it has reached viability. All our campus pastors are looking for potential campus pastors within their congregations from the first day their campus opens.

The transmission for the rapidly expanding multi-site church is the distribution system. How do you get the goods to the campus? This includes everything a campus needs to do ministry on a day-to-day basis. The less the staff has to worry about how the goods are going to get there, the more effective they will be at doing ministry. As you create a delivery system, it's important to think about scalability. When Life Church added a satellite dish in Edmond, it wasn't thinking just about how to get the video message to Oklahoma City, Tulsa, and Stillwater; it was thinking about delivering the message to sites all over the country. One of the major keys to the success of Wal-Mart had very little to do with low prices or great service; Wal-Mart solved the distribution puzzle better than anyone else in the world.

The third essential part of replication is having a good owner's manual—making sure that whatever you do in opening a campus is documented and repeatable. At Seacoast, we make checklists of everything that we do when opening a campus, and we work through the lists systematically. Our equipment is nearly identical from campus to campus. We have a standard "package" that we place at each new location. We are fanatical about making lists of everything we buy so that we don't have to reinvent the wheel. The more you document your first and second campus openings, the easier the third, fourth, and beyond will be.

The real power of the multi-site revolution is not simply in opening a second or even a third location; the power begins as churches get a vision for five sites, ten sites, and a reproducing movement of campuses that cross regional and cultural boundaries, reaching people well beyond the four walls of the original campus. Dave Browning of Christ the King in Washington describes the power like this: "People see our signs in several different communities and start to get the picture that we are here for them. People in nearby communities hear about us before we get there. People who attend Christ the King in one location will invite friends who live in another community to check out Christ the King there. And when a family moves from one community to another, it's not a loss to our church—it's a transfer."

> As church leaders begin to see beyond what they once thought was possible, they begin to experience the power of revolutionary multiplication.

Just a Fad? Will the Multi-Site Movement Last?

Perhaps the best vote about the durability of the multi-site movement should come from the track record of the pioneers. A few U.S. churches have been multi-site for fifty to one hundred years. The sprinkling of churches becoming multi-site began turning into a trickle about twenty years ago and into a stream starting three to five years ago. Will the stream continue to build?

Bob Cottingham, pastor of North Heights Lutheran Church in greater Minneapolis, serves a church that has been multi-site since 1986. It had maxed out its original site, trying to accommodate six times as many people for worship each weekend as it had seats. So it added a second campus seven miles away. "Previously, it was turmoil every weekend. We wouldn't have maintained our size and growth at our original site, and we would have gone into maintenance mode," Bob affirms.

"Multi-site churches are not a fad," he continues. "They are most likely the wave of the future." Why? "The multi-site approach will last because it has the ability to offer a stable and successful start at another site without having to create a whole new church. The financial base, staffing relationships, and proven church leadership are just extended to another site. It is not hit or miss."

North Heights, with two decades of experience, has seen some of the problems that occur if a church's campuses don't work together. "The most significant adjustments for us has been the breaking of silos," Bob says. "Every ministry at both sites must communicate with each other if the two sites are to move ahead together." But he has also seen the long-term fruit of multi-site as the model matures. "Churches that want to change their cities cannot afford to be in maintenance mode," he says.

In that sense, the cycle of replication has barely begun for North Heights.

Where Do We Go from Here?

Be part of turning the tide in a battle being lost by current approaches to doing church

> Now, compelled by the Spirit, I am going to Jerusalem, not knowing what will happen to me there. — Acts 20:22

After opening Seacoast's first off-site campus in April 2002, we (Geoff) were approached by a church we had helped plant four years earlier. It wanted to become our second videocast campus. We immediately noted several seemingly insurmountable obstacles: the church was in a terrible location, its attendance was stagnant, it had a very different style of service from Seacoast's, and it was located one hundred miles away.

So we said, "Yes, certainly." We put together a new band, redecorated their facility, changed their children's program, and installed new lighting, video, and audio systems. In preparation for the grand opening, we purchased ads on secular radio stations, bought space in the local newspaper, and sent out 40,000 flyers inviting people to the "Grand Opening" of Seacoast Church—Columbia, South Carolina.

(Geography trivia: Columbia is one hundred miles away from the closest "seacoast.")

When the grand opening arrived, the building was packed. Every seat was filled, and people were standing along the walls. The band was hot, the worship leader incredible, and everything else was awesome.

Then it came time for the big test: how would people react to teaching on video by a preacher one hundred miles away? We started the DVD, and within a few minutes, the entire audience was engaged. They were reading the Scriptures out loud when asked to by the preacher, laughing at the jokes, and filling out their note sheets. "This multi-site thing might actually work," we whispered to each other.

Then the teaching pastor froze. Literally. There on the giant screen the speaker had gone into suspended animation. In the tech booth, I was frantically trying to get the DVD to begin playing again. After what seemed like hours (only a few seconds I was later told), our prerecorded pastor resumed his sermon. With a sigh of relief, I began to survey the damage. Amazingly, people were reengaging with the message.

Then he froze again. But this time he was quivering like a bowl of flesh-colored Jell-O. Plus his lips had left his face and were now located just above his left shoulder, and his lips were quivering as well! In a cold sweat, I once again tried to resurrect the DVD, but to no avail. The virtual pastor would not be completing his message—all he could do was tremble in vain, trying to retrieve his mouth. After a few minutes of tense silence, the campus pastor took the stage and mumbled an apology, assuring everyone that we would have this fixed by the next week.

I assumed that the multi-site was dead and that I was unemployed.

We had church the next weekend just to see if anyone would show up. They did! Most of the people from the weekend before returned. They said they liked the worship, they felt helped by the part of the message they had heard, and they were drawn to the warmth of the congregation.

> I assumed that the multi-site was dead and that I was unemployed.

They understood that technical glitches happen, and they were willing to give us a second chance.

I'm so glad we serve a God of second chances.

He kept working through headstrong Peter, doubting Thomas, and impatient James and John. Yes, the Holy Spirit worked through those people who "failed," spreading the gospel across the globe, reaching me six thousand miles and almost two thousand years later. Likewise, today God has somehow decided to bless his church through the occasionally inept leadership of Seacoast. As Scripture says, "I planted the seed, Apollos watered it, but God made it grow" (1 Cor. 3:6).

Joe Aldrich opens his book, *Lifestyle Evangelism*, with an imaginary conversation between Jesus and the angel Gabriel in heaven. It takes place just after Jesus' resurrection. Gabriel was astounded that God would entrust a small band of very fallible human beings with the task of spreading the gospel to the entire world. Shaking his head at the thought, Gabriel says, in effect, "What if they don't come through?" Jesus then offers a sober reply: "I have no other plan. I'm counting on them."[1]

No Formulas, No Restrictions

Now it's two thousand years later, and the American church is running out of steam when it comes to spreading the good news. We have become effective at moving the already convinced from one church to another, while building larger and larger ministries. Yet there are more unchurched people in America now than at any previous time in our history. We must continually seek culturally relevant ways to reach more people with Jesus' message of love and hope.

The exciting news is that some churches are doing just that. The impact of multi-site churches is exploding as the "way we've always done it" is being expanded into new avenues of ministry. As effective evangelistic churches open new venues and campuses, new people are being reached that otherwise might never have been touched by a church.

> Yet there are more unchurched people in America now than at any previous time in our history.

For churches of all sizes, opening a new campus has become an incredible tool for evangelism. As with anything new, there's an excitement in the air, a passion from the campus pastor and the core team to reach out to new people, to reach the lost. Members who have been on the sidelines at the existing church become fired up about the new work in their neighborhood, and they step into the front lines. They begin to invite their friends, their neighbors, their relatives to check out the new church. Life change happens as people experience the good news of the gospel in a fresh and relevant way. Churches report that in the majority of new sites, the level of evangelism is greatly increased.

Churches that are in decline are beginning to see the multi-site movement as an opportunity for a fresh start. Rather than dying a slow death of attrition as members move away, leave, or die, these congregations are merging with growing churches in their area and becoming off-site campuses. New life is pumped into these ministries as once again people are committing their lives to Christ, and neighborhoods are being revitalized as these newly energized congregations once again turn their focus outward. Rather than becoming restaurants and office buildings, church buildings are once again becoming life-giving stations in their communities.

As multi-site churches continue to expand, they are crossing boundaries, both physical and perceived. Churches are beginning to open cross-cultural campuses in neighborhoods very different from their primary campuses. They are putting resources into needy areas that fast-growing churches have often bypassed. How? Suburban churches are returning to the city and opening campuses in neighborhoods they left years before. New campuses are opening up in smaller towns and rural settings as well.

Multi-site is more than a strategy to get big.

Campuses are being planted internationally, breaking down barriers of language and style and going into countries where traditional mission efforts have struggled.

Multi-site is more than a strategy to get big. Many churches are becoming smaller as they open microcampuses. Churches are going into firehouses, jails, and senior centers and offering through video, to five, ten, twenty people at a time, the same level of excellence that is found in the large primary campus. House churches are leveraging the power of multi-site churches to provide effective teaching for their congregations. Churches have begun adding campus pastors for their Internet congregations as people are committing their lives to Christ through online connections.

The possibilities for spreading the gospel and impacting communities through multi-site ministry are endless. One scenario involves leveraging neighborhood theaters. As cinemas across the country are being upgraded with high-definition digital video projectors and are linked by satellite to content providers, churches will soon be able to broadcast their weekend services to any theater in America. Services could run every hour or even every half hour any day of the week. Different churches could use the same theater at the same time, broadcasting on different screens. New believers could be connected in virtual communities, learning and growing as they connect with other believers in their own neighborhood, across the country, and around the world. Resources could be focused on reaching the lost, feeding the poor, and changing communities rather than on buying land and building buildings. Multi-site could eventually change the location people picture when they answer the question, "What is a church?"

Jesus left the church with one final instruction: make disciples, baptize, and teach. The apostle Paul was so committed to fulfilling that mission that he constantly looked for new and innovative ways to spread the gospel. He told the church at Corinth:

> To the Jews I became like a Jew, to win the Jews. To those under the law I became like one under the law (though I myself am not under the law), so as to win those under the law. To those not having the law I became like one not having the law (though I am not free from God's law but am under Christ's law), so as to win those not having the law. To the weak I became weak, to win the weak. I have become all things to all men so that by all possible means I might save some.

1 Corinthians 9:20–22

The churches in the first century were not defined by a building or a location. Groups of believers met in homes, in synagogues, and in the open air. When they faced persecution, they changed location and continued worshiping together. They did not think of themselves as distinct communities competing for members; they saw themselves as part of the whole, each one building up the others. The church at Corinth, the church at Antioch, and the church at Ephesus all considered themselves part of one church with one mission: to reach the world for Christ. That single-minded commitment revolutionized their world.

> Multi-site could eventually change the location people picture when they answer the question, "What is a church?"

The future of the multi-site church might be a return to the mindset of the first-century believer, when the word *church* did not refer to a specific building or location but to a group of believers connected to other groups of believers by a common mission. *Imagine the power of a church not built around a personality or a facility but instead built around a mission!* Wherever two or three believers gather, there could be a new campus. Churches could meet in homes, in coffee shops, in break rooms at work. Resources could be directed at spreading the gospel and meeting the needs of the community rather than at more land and bigger buildings. Church might no longer be thought of as an hour on Sunday or a visit to a building. Church might become a lifestyle lived every day in every place the believer walks. Megachurches could become resources for smaller bodies of believers, providing teaching content, oversight, and accountability. While this may be a utopian view, it reflects what we read of the first-century believers in Acts 2.

> The church at Corinth, the church at Antioch, and the church at Ephesus all considered themselves part of one church with one mission: to reach the world for Christ.

All the believers were together and had everything in common. Selling their possessions and goods, they gave to anyone as he had need. Every day they continued to meet together in the temple courts. They broke bread in their homes and ate together with glad and sincere hearts, praising God and enjoying the favor of all the people. And the Lord added to their number daily those who were being saved.

ACTS 2:44–47

If we are to truly go into all the world and make disciples of all the nations, we can no longer hold on to the comfortable thought of being a church that meets in one location under one roof. Empowered by God's Holy Spirit, we must cross boundaries into other neighborhoods and cultures. We have to open our doors to other churches that may be more effective at reaching the lost and making disciples than we are. We need to put aside our preconceptions of what a church is, what a pastor is, or how the good news should be delivered. And when we do so, it will be said of us that we too have turned the world upside down.

Internet Link for Multi-Site Toolbox

Appendix A

The workouts at the end of chapters 3 – 8 are a great way to start putting this book to practical use. If you haven't seriously reflected on them, do take the time to benefit from them.

The following Internet link will carry you even further. Go to **www.multisitechurchrevolution.com** and click the "Multi-Site Toolkit" link in the upper right. There you will find the best tools we have found at multi-site churches across the country: role profiles, organizational charts, launch checklists, evaluation tools, and more.

International Multi-Site Overview

Appendix B

A multi-site church, according to chapter 1 of this book, "is one church meeting in multiple locations — different rooms on the same campus, different locations in the same region, or in some instances, different cities, states, or nations. A multi-site church shares a common vision, budget, leadership, and board."

The largest church in the history of Christendom, whose pastor and majority of members are converts from Buddhist and Shamanist backgrounds, uses a multi-site approach to reach people for Christ. The Yoido Full Gospel Church, pastored by David Yonggi Cho, is located in Seoul, Korea. Its ten weekly services draw 150,000 people to the five-building campus, itself a multi-venue setting involving a 12,000-seat main sanctuary plus seating for 20,000 others in twenty-two chapels, all connected by closed-circuit television. Some fifty satellite churches around the perimeter of Seoul help accommodate the remaining congregation.

Churches like Yoido Full Gospel are way ahead of churches in North America in developing multi-site ministry. Joel Comiskey, author of several books on cell churches and leadership-development models around the world, mentions several of the following multi-site churches in his report on worldwide cell churches.[1]

- In Abidjan, Ivory Coast, pastor Dion Robert's cell church, The Works and Mission Baptist Church, meets in hundreds of satellite churches that consist of 150,000 people with only 6,000 meeting in any one place.[2]
- In Lisbon, Portugal, Igreja Mana Church, pastored by George Tadeau, involves 60,000 people in worship services through 400 satellite churches.
- In Bombay, India, 50,000 people worship weekly through 250 satellite churches connected with New Life Fellowship, pastored by S. Joseph.
- In Sydney, Australia, Hillsong Church, where Brian Houston is pastor and Darlene Zschech is worship director, has become multi-site in recent years.

The multi-site approach can also be found in Ghana, South Africa, Brazil, Chile, Argentina, Ecuador, and elsewhere.

In a development rich in symbolism, Africa's largest evangelical church, the Nigeria-based Redeemed Christian Church of God, has come to the United States, building its North American headquarters an hour's drive northeast of Dallas. With a worldwide membership of more than 2 million people, the movement has congregations in 90 countries including the United States, which has some 300 churches to date. The movement's mission statement includes having a church within a five-minute walk of every city in developing countries and within a five-minute drive in a developed nation.

If Redeemed Christian follows the course of many other fast-growing international churches, it will take on a multi-site character, and the ripple effect will further influence how the rest of us do church here in North America.

Directory of Multi-Site Churches Cited

Appendix C

As stated in the preface, we predict that 30,000 American churches will be doing multi-site within the next few years, which means one or more multi-site churches will probably be in your area. The following list contains only the multi-site churches cited in this book, but if you ask around, you're certain to learn about more.

The first column in the table on the following pages indicates whether the main teaching at the primary church's venues and satellite locations is by video (V), in person (P), or a combination of both (B). All data in the table is current as of January 2006.

Directory of Multi-Site Churches Cited

Teaching*	Church Name	City	State	Senior Pastor	Website
B	Bethlehem Baptist Church	Minneapolis	MN	John Piper	www.bbcmpls.org
V	Blackhawk Church	Madison	WI	Chris Dolson	www.blackhawkchurch.org
V	Brethren in Christ Church	Carlisle	PA	Alan Robinson	www.carlislebic.org
P	Chartwell Baptist Church	Oakwood (Toronto)	ON	Peter Roebbelen	www.chartwellchurch.org
B	Christ Fellowship	Palm Beach Gardens	FL	Tom Mullins	www.gochristfellowship.com
B	Christ the King Community Church	Mount Vernon	WA	Dave Browning	www.ctkonline.com
B	Colorado Community Church	Englewood	CO	Anthony Pranno	www.coloradocommunity.org
B	Community Christian Church	Naperville (Chicago)	IL	Dave Ferguson	www.communitychristian.org
V	Community Presbyterian Church	Danville	CA	Scott Farmer	www.cpcdanville.org
P	Eastern Star (Baptist) Church	Indianapolis	IN	Jeffrey Johnson	www.easternstarchurch.org
P	Evergreen Community Church	Burnsville (Minneapolis)	MN	Brent Knox	www.evergreencc.com
V	Fellowship Bible Church	Little Rock	AK	Tim Lundy	www.fbclr.com
V	Fellowship Church	Grapevine (Dallas)	TX	Ed Young, Jr.	www.fellowshipchurch.com
P	First Baptist Church	Windermere	FL	Mark Matheson	www.fbcwindermere.com
B	First United Methodist Church	Sedalia	MO	Jim Downing	www.firstsayyes.com

* Codes for teaching and preaching column (referring to venues and satellite locations): V = video; P = in person; B = various combinations of both

Teaching*	Church Name	City	State	Senior Pastor	Website
P	First United Methodist Church	Van Alstyne	TX	John Gondol	www.vanalstynefumc.org
P	The Fountain of Praise	Houston	TX	Remus Wright	www.fountainofpraise.org
P	Franklin Avenue Baptist Church	New Orleans	LA	Fred Luter Jr.	www.franklinabc.com
B	Grace Community Church	Tyler	TX	Doug Clark	www.gcc.org
B	Gulf Breeze United Methodist Church	Gulf Breeze (Pensacola)	FL	Mack Strange	www.gbumc.org
B	Harvest Bible Chapel	Rolling Meadows	IL	James MacDonald	www.harvestbible.org
V	Healing Place Church	Baton Rouge	LA	Dino Rizzo	www.healingplacechurch.org
V	Heartland Community Church	Rockford	IL	Doug Thiesen	www.heartland.cc
P	Immanuel United Methodist Church	Lakeside Park	KY	Barry Carpenter	www.immanuelumc.org
B	Jacksonville Chapel	Lincoln Park	NJ	Dave Gustavsen	www.jacksonvillechapel.org
V	Lake Pointe Church	Rockwall (Dallas)	TX	Steve Stroope	www.lakepointe.org
V	LifeChurch.tv	Oklahoma City	OK	Craig Groeschel	www.lifechurch.tv
P	Mosaic	City of Industry (Los Angeles)	CA	Erwin McManus	www.mosaic.org
P	Mount Zion Baptist Church	White Creek	TN	Joseph Walker III	www.mtzionnashville.org
V	Nappanee Missionary Church	Nappanee	IN	Dave Engbrecht	www.nmc1.org
V	National Community Church	Washington	D.C.	Mark Batterson	www.theaterchurch.com

	Church	City	State	Teaching/Preaching	Website
P	New Birth Missionary Baptist Church	Lithonia	GA	Eddie Long	www.newbirth.org
B	New Hope Christian Fellowship	Honolulu	HI	Wayne Cordeiro	www.enewhope.org
P	New Life Church	West Linn (Portland)	OR	Scott Reavely	www.newlifenw.com
B	New Life Community Church	Chicago	IL	Mark Jobe	www.newlifechicago.org
B	NewSong Church	Irvine	CA	Dave Gibbons	www.newsong.net
B	North Coast Church	Vista	CA	Larry Osborne	www.northcoastchurch.com
B	North Heights Lutheran	Roseville (Minneapolis)	MN	Bob Cottingham	www.nhlc.org
V	North Point Community Church	Alpharetta (Atlanta)	GA	Andy Stanley	www.northpoint.org
V	Northland—A Church Distributed	Longwood	FL	Joel Hunter	www.northlandcc.net
P	Olathe Bible Church	Olathe	KS	Rex Bonar	www.olathebible.org
V	Potter's House	Dallas	TX	T. D. Jakes	www.thepottershouse.org
P	Redeemer Presbyterian	New York	NY	Tim Keller	www.redeemer.com
B	RockPointe Church	Calgary	BC	Brent Trask	www.bvalliance.ca
P	Rutgers Community Christian Church	Somerset	NJ	Caleb Huang	www.rccc.org
V	Saddleback Church	Lake Forest	CA	Rick Warren	www.saddleback.com
B	St. Luke's United Methodist Church	Indianapolis	IN	Kent Millard	www.stlukesumc.com
B	Seacoast Church	Mount Pleasant	SC	Greg Surratt	www.seacoastchurch.org

* Codes for teaching and preaching column (referring to venues and satellite locations): V = video; P = in person; B = various combinations of both

Teaching*	Church Name	City	State	Senior Pastor	Website
B	Second Baptist Church	Houston	TX	Edwin Young	www.second.org
P	Southeast Christian Church	Louisville	KY	Bob Russell	www.southeastchristian.org
P	Southside Community Church	Surrey	BC	Cam Roxburgh	www.southside.ca
V	Stillwater United Methodist Church	Dayton	OH	Duane Anders	www.stillwaterumc.org
P	The Chapel	Akron	OH	Knute Larson	www.the-chapel.org
P	The Journey	New York	NY	Nelson Searcy	www.nyjourney.com
V	Willow Creek Community Church	South Barrington (Chicago)	IL	Bill Hybels	www.willowcreek.org
B	Without Walls International Church	Tampa	FL	Randy White	www.withoutwalls.org
V	World Changers Church International	College Park	GA	Creflo Dollar	www.worldchangers.org

* Codes for teaching and preaching column (referring to venues and satellite locations): V = video; P = in person; B = various combinations of both

Acknowledgments

This book is dedicated to:

- God — you are the author of all truth, the driver of all movements, and the recipient of all praise that this work may receive.
- Lyle Schaller, Carl George, Elmer Towns, and John Vaughan — you are the conceptual pioneers who have prophetically been speaking for many years about the efficacy of multi-site churches.
- The many churches featured in this book, especially those that have been a part of Leadership Network's Multi-Site Churches Leadership Community — you are the practitioner pioneers that have taken multi-site from concept to revolution.
- Dave Travis, Warren Schuh, and Linda Stanley — you were the Leadership Network advance scouts who listened well and convened the first anointed practitioners who have led the movement.
- Julia Burk and Stephanie Plagens — you are the scribes who have tirelessly helped us make sure that all the t's were crossed and i's dotted. You have graciously worked with each featured church to make sure its information is accurate and its story told in a way they feel represents them well.
- Bob Buford, Tom Wilson, Gayle Carpenter, and the rest of the Leadership Network team — you are the partners whose generosity and leadership have enabled us to fulfill a portion of the Leadership Network mission of helping high-capacity leaders multiply their impact in a unique way.

All weaknesses in the book are our own fault, but many strengths can be attributed to our colleagues who commented on the manuscript at various stages: Chip Arn, D. J. Chuang, Ellen and Mark Frisius, Jack Hoey, Billy Hornsby, Josh Hunt, Don Jaques, Pam Joyce, Scott Reavely, Scott Thumma, and Steve Yarrow. You are the eyes and ears that helped us turn raw ideas into powerful thoughts that we pray will serve to further fuel the multi-site church revolution.

We want to express particular appreciation to our wives and families. You are our companions whose presence, encouragement, and sacrifice have provided the space required to make this contribution to the multi-site movement.

Finally, we appreciate the partnership of Zondervan, both Mark Sweeney as our publishing liaison and Paul Engle as our primary editor. This book, along with Mark Driscoll's book, *Confessions of a Reformission Rev.: Hard Lessons from an Emerging Missional Church*, mark the inaugural volumes of the Leadership Network Innovation Series, which we trust will be a rich trove of resources in building God's kingdom.

Notes

Chapter : Preface

1. This finding comes from a list of churches compiled by Leadership Network. The churches cited in this book are listed in appendix C. In personal conversation (8/10/05), noted church researcher Elmer Towns responded to our "1,500 multi-site churches" statement as follows: "It all depends on how you define 'multi-site.' If you mean multi-worship services on Sunday morning at a separate site, many more than one thousand churches are doing multi-site work. But if you define multi-site to include nursing home services, prison services, mission Sunday schools and/or chapels, then probably the number one thousand is extremely small."

2. Hartford Institute for Religion Research and Leadership Network, "Megachurch 2005 Survey," http://www.hirr.hartsem.edu. This survey states that 27 percent of megachurches are "holding services at multiple locations."

3. Thom Rainer, "One Church, Two Locations," *Outreach* 4, no. 4 (July/August 2005): 18, http://www.outreach.com. Rainer's wording is that these churches have "moved or probably would be moving" in the direction of a multi-campus model. He also notes that only 5 percent indicated the same interest two years earlier.

4. See "America's Ten Fastest-Growing Churches" and "America's Ten Largest Churches," tables in chapter 1 of this book, pages 22–23.

5. Andrew Wood, "Wal-Mart of the Hospitality World," *Motel Americana*, http://www2.sjsu.edu/faculty/wooda/motel/holiday.

6. Bob Smietana, "High-Tech Circuit Riders," *Christianity Today* 49, no. 9 (September 2005): 60, http://www.christianitytoday.com/ct/2005/009/24.60.html.

7. Dave Ferguson, "The Multi-Site Church: Some of the Strengths of This New Life Form," *Leadership Journal*, Spring 2003: 81.

8. Patrick Kampert, "God (Trade Mark)," *Chicago Tribune*, January 16, 2005, http://www.chicagotribune.com.

9. Jeff Mosier, "Lake Pointe: Two Flocks Linked by High Technology," *Dallas Morning News*, January 1, 2004, http://www.dallasnews.com; Linda Stewart Ball, "Fellowship Extends Its Reach with Two Satellite Campuses," *Dallas Morning News*, January 15, 2005, http://www.dallasnews.com.

10. "Cineplex Church," *Religion and Ethics Newsweekly*, episode 539, May 31, 2002, http://www.pbs.org/wnet/religionandethics/week539/feature.html (accessed September 1, 2005).

11. Petra Mayer, *All Things Considered*, NPR, August 7, 2005, http://www.npr.org/templates/story/story.php?storyId=4788676.

12. W. Charles Arn, *How to Start a New Service: Your Church Can Reach New People.* (Grand Rapids: Baker, 1997), back cover.

Chapter One: You Say You Want a Revolution?

1. Elmer Towns, *Ten of Today's Most Innovative Churches: What They're Doing, How They're Doing It and How You Can Apply Their Ideas in Your Church*, (Ventura: Regal, 1990), 242–43. Although the book is out of print, it is currently available at no charge at http://www.elmertowns.com.

2. Aubrey Malphurs, *Being Leaders: The Nature of Authentic Christian Leadership*, (Grand Rapids: Baker, 2003), 22–26. *Being Leaders* is the first book in a trilogy that

Malphurs has written on leadership. *Leading Leaders: Empowering Church Boards for Ministry Excellence* (Grand Rapids: Baker, 2005), 32–35, a book for church governing boards (and second in the trilogy), also addresses the house- and city-church phenomenon.

3. Towns, *Ten of Today's Most Innovative Churches*, 239.

4. The Louisville Institute, http://www.louisville-institute.org (the report itself is not available online).

5. Hartford Institute, "Megachurch 2005 Survey."

6. Capella Tucker, *All Things Considered*, NPR, July 18, 2005, http://www.npr.org/tem plates/story/story.php?storyId=4759649.

7. Bill Easum and Dave Travis, *Beyond the Box: Innovative Churches That Work* (Loveland, CO: Group, 2003), 85.

8. Barna Research Group, "Number of Unchurched Adults Has Nearly Doubled Since 1991," May 4, 2004, http://www.barna.org. Since 1991, the adult population in the United States has grown by 15 percent. During that same period, the number of adults who do not attend church has nearly doubled, rising from 39 million to 75 million—a 92 percent increase!

9. Rainer, "One Church, Two Locations," 18.

Chapter Two: A Wide Variety of Models

1. Arn, *How to Start a New Service*, back cover.

Chapter Three: Would It Work for You?

1. Dave Ferguson, "The Multi-Site Church," *Leadership Journal*, Spring 2003, 81–84, http://www.christianitytoday.com/le/2003/002/21.81.html. See also Eric Reed, "Let's Go to the Tape," *Leadership Journal*, Spring 2003, 76–80, http://www.christianitytoday.com/le/2003/002/20.76.html.

2. James C. Collins and Jerry I. Porras, *Built to Last: Successful Habits of Visionary Companies* (New York: HarperBusiness, 2002), 43–45.

Chapter Four: On a Mission from God

1. For more information on the "One Big Idea" approach, popularized by Community Christian Church, Chicago, Illinois, see http://www.communitychristian.org; and "Multi-Site Special Report," Leadership Network, http://www.leadnet.org/store/down loads.asp.

2. For more on this story, see Linda McCoy, *Planting a Garden: Growing the Church Beyond Traditional Models* (Nashville: Abingdon, 2005).

Chapter Five: Opportunity Knocks

1. Rez Gopez-Sindac, "The C.E. Interview," *Church Executive Magazine*, September 2005, http://www.churchexecutive.com/2005/09/The_CE_Interview_Larry_Osborne_ Senior_Pastor_North_Coast_Church_Vista_CA.asp.

2. See "America's Ten Fastest-Growing Churches" and "America's Ten Largest-Attendance Churches," tables in chapter 1 of this book, pages 22–23.

Chapter Six: Selling the Dream

1. Lyle E. Schaller, *Activating the Passive Church: Diagnosis and Treatment* (Nashville: Abingdon, 1981).

2. Ferguson, "The Multi-Site Church," 81.

3. Easum and Travis, *Beyond the Box*, 89.

4. Robert Lewis and Wayne Cordeiro with Warren Bird, *Culture Shift: Transforming Your Church from the Inside Out* (San Francisco: Jossey-Bass, 2005).

5. Ibid., 164–65. MacDonald discusses the traits of a "VDP" in Gordon MacDonald, *Restoring Your Spiritual Passion* (Nashville: Thomas Nelson, 1986), 71–91.

Chapter Seven: Who's Going to Pay for This?

1. For an architectural history of U.S. worship facilities from the colonial era to the present, see Anne C. Loveland and Otis B. Wheeler, *From Meetinghouse to Megachurch: A Material and Cultural History* (St. Louis: University of Missouri Press, 2003).

2. See Ray Bowman and Eddy Hall, *When Not to Build: An Architect's Unconventional Wisdom for the Growing Church* (Grand Rapids: Baker, 2000); Ray Oldenburg, *The Great Good Place* (New York: Marlowe & Company, 1999).

3. Bill Easum and Pete Theodore, *The Nomadic Church: Growing Your Congregation without Owning the Building* (Nashville: Abingdon, 2005), 17. See also Ralph D. Curtin, *Sharing Your Church Building* (Grand Rapids: Baker, 2002).

Chapter Eight: Launching the Mission

1. Consider also these audio conferences: Mark Bankord, Dave Ferguson, and Jim Tomberlin, "The Multi-Site Church," *Defining Moments* (Willow Creek Association's monthly audio journal); Willow Creek Multi-Site Forum, August 10, 2005, http://www .willowcreek.com/CGI-BIN/texis.exe/webinator/search?pageID=1&sectionID=1&pr =default&prox=page&rorder=750&rprox=750&rdfreq=250&rwfreq=500&rlead=10 00&sufs=2&order=r&query=multi-site&cqBoxes=1&cqBoxes=2&cqBoxes=3&cqBox es=4&cqBoxes=5]; "Multi-Site Conference," October 24–25, 2005, Naperville, IL, www .multi-site.org.

2. Elmer L. Towns and Douglas Porter, *Churches That Multiply: A Bible Study on Church Planting* (Kansas City, MO: Nazarene, 2003).

3. Bill Easum and Pete Theodore, *The Nomadic Church: Growing Your Congregation without Owning the Building* (Nashville: Abingdon, 2005).

4. Dale Galloway with Warren Bird, *Starting a New Church: How to Plant a High-Impact Congregation* (Kansas City: Beacon Hill Press, 2003), with accompanying DVD.

5. Ed Stetzer, *Planting New Churches in a Postmodern Age* (Nashville: Broadman & Holman, 2003).

6. Lyle E. Schaller, *44 Questions for Church Planters* (Nashville: Abingdon, 1991).

7. Peter C. Wagner, *Church Planting for a Greater Harvest: A Comprehensive Guide* (Ventura, CA: Regal, 1990).

8. Cindi Haworth, ed., *Church Planting Resources: A Comprehensive, Annotated Guide, 2005 Edition*, Leadership Network, 2005, http://www.leadnet.org/downloads.asp.

Chapter Nine: Hitting the Sweet Spot

1. See also Warren Bird, "Not Your Mama's Church: A Multi-Ethnic Movement to Reach Leaders of the Next Generation," *Leadership Journal* 25, no. 4 (Fall 2004):11, http:// www.christianitytoday.com/le/2004/004/11.11.html.

2. Peter F. Drucker, "Your Leadership Is Unique," *Leadership Journal* 17, no. 4, (Fall 1996): 54, http://www.christianitytoday.com/bcl/areas/leadership/articles/ le–6l4–6l4054.html.

Chapter Eleven: Building Better Leaders

1. The Mark Jobe quotes in this section come from "Unlikely Candidates," *Leadership Journal*, Summer 2003, http://www.christianitytoday.com/le/2003/003/6.46.html. Used by permission. The material is slightly edited by permission of the author, and new facts have been added. See also the story of Mark Jobe's church in Michael Pocock and Joseph Henriques, *Cultural Change and Your Church* (Grand Rapids: Baker, 2002), 179–92.

2. Fred Smith Sr., excerpted with permission from *Leadership Weekly*, a newsletter from the editors of *Leadership Journal*, November 18, 2003 and November 25, 2003, http://www.christianitytoday.com/leaders/newsletter/2003/cln31118.html.

3. Carl George with Warren Bird, *Nine Keys to Effective Small-Group Leadership*. (Mansfield, PA: Kingdom, 1997), 47.

4. Ibid., 46, 68.

5. James Noel, *Action Learning: How the World's Top Companies Are Re-Creating Their Leaders and Themselves* (San Francisco: Jossey-Bass, 1998).

6. Adapted from *Leadership Network Explorer* no. 52, December 2001, http://www.leadnet.org.

7. Ram Charan, James L. Noel, and Stephen Drotter, *Leadership Pipeline: How to Build the Leadership-Powered Company* (Hoboken, NJ: Wiley, 2000).

Chapter Twelve: Leveraging Technology

1. Bobby Ross Jr, "Tech-Savvy Megachurches Expand with Big Screens on 'Satellite Campuses,'" *ReligionJournal.com*, June 30, 2005, http://www.religionjournal.com/show-article.asp?id=2746.

Chapter Thirteen: Avoiding Detours

1. Jerry Graham, "A Strategy and Template for the Addition of New Satellites for New Life Christian Fellowship," (D.Min. dissertation, Fuller Theological Seminary, May 2001). Available online at http://www.vanguardministries.org/pdf/satellite_strategy.pdf.

2. For a fuller account of how Ginghamsburg is investing in its relationship with Medway, see Mike Slaughter with Warren Bird and Kim Miller, *Momentum for Life* (Nashville, TN: Abingdon, 2005), 109–10.

3. Michael Slaughter with Warren Bird, *UnLearning Church: Just When You Thought You Had Leadership All Figured Out!* (Loveland, CO: Group, 2002), 25.

Chapter Fourteen: Secrets of Ongoing Replication

1. Dave Ferguson, "The Reproducing Church," Building Church Leaders series published by Christianity Today, Inc., August 10, 2005, http://www.christianitytoday.com/bcl/areas/vision-strategy/articles/081005.html

Chapter Fifteen: Where Do We Go from Here?

1. Joe Aldrich, *Lifestyle Evangelism: Learning to Open Your Life to Those Around You* (Portland, OR: Multnomah, 1999), 15.

Apendix B: International Multi-Site Overview

1. Joel Comiskey, "Ten Largest Cell Churches," *Cell Group Journal*, December 2000, http://www.touchusa.org/cellchurch/magfiles/10.1.asp. See also Joel's books *Cell Church Solutions* and *Reap the Harvest*, both available at http://www.comiskey.com.

2. Les Brickman, "Rapid Cell Church Growth and Reproduction: Case Study of Eglise Protestante Baptiste Oeuvres et Mission Internationale, Abidjan, Cote D'Ivoire," (D. Min. dissertation, Regent University, November 2000).

Scripture Index

Subject Index

Note: Page numbers in italics refer to tables. Page numbers with an *n* refer to endnotes.

About the Authors

Geoff Surratt is on the executive management team of Seacoast Church, a multi-site congregation that has expanded from one to nine locations since he joined the staff in 1996 (and overall attendance has grown from 1,000 to 7,000). As campus-development pastor, he oversees the current campuses and also the planning efforts to expand to a dozen more campuses in the near future. He also directs a large-church multi-site leadership community for Leadership Network. Geoff speaks regularly at multi-site training conferences, and in his spare time, he enjoys hang gliding and mountain climbing, though his extreme fear of heights severely limits his involvement in either activity. Geoff has twenty-two years of ministry experience in a variety of roles in local churches. He graduated from Southwestern Assemblies of God University with a bachelor's degree in general ministry. He is married to Sherry, and they have two children, Mike and Brittainy. They live in Charleston, South Carolina.

Greg Ligon has spent the last four years pioneering and building a network of more than fifty multi-site churches on behalf of Leadership Network. These networks are known as leadership communities and involve each church making a two-year commitment to share with its peers what it learns. Greg's role involves ongoing dialogue with each church to track its progress and needs, as well as making numerous visits to multi-site congregations. Greg frequently speaks at multi-site training conferences. A capable writer and editor, Greg is also director of publishing for Leadership Network. Before joining the Leadership Network team, Greg launched and directed the United Methodist Campus Ministry at Southern Methodist University in Dallas for seven years. He also served as associate pastor at First United Methodist Church in Waco, Texas, for two years. He did his undergraduate work at Texas Tech University and graduated from Asbury Theological Seminary. He is married to Susan, has two "high-octane" boys, Daniel and Andrew, and lives in Dallas, Texas.

Warren Bird serves as the research director and as a primary writer for Leadership Network. He has been researching multi-site churches for years, bringing the idea of the multi-site church to publishers and being rejected three times because it was "too soon." He has worshiped with and conducted on-site interviews at several dozen multi-site churches across the country. An accomplished author, he has collaboratively written fifteen books and almost two hundred magazine articles, all on subjects of church health or church innovation. One book, collaboratively authored for Pete Scazzero, won the prestigious Gold Medallion award—*Emotionally Healthy Church* (Zondervan). He has been an adjunct seminary professor for ten years. He served for ten years on staff part-time at a multi-venue church in Princeton, New Jersey. He graduated from Wheaton College, Wheaton Graduate School, and Alliance Theological Seminary. He is a Ph.D. student with specialization in megachurches. He is married and has two grown children. Warren and his wife, Michelle, live just outside New York City.

About the Leadership Network Innovation Series

Since 1984, Leadership Network has fostered church innovation and growth by diligently pursuing its far-reaching mission statement: *To identify high-capacity Christian leaders, to connect them with other leaders, and to help them multiply their impact.*

While specific techniques may vary as the church faces new opportunities and challenges, Leadership Network consistently focuses on bringing together entrepreneurial leaders who are pursuing similar ministry initiatives. The resulting peer-to-peer interaction, dialogue, and collaboration—often across denominational lines—helps these leaders better refine their individual strategies and accelerate their own innovations.

To further enhance this process, Leadership Network develops and distributes highly targeted ministry tools and resources, including books, DVDs and videotapes, special reports, e-publications, and free downloads.

Launched in 2006, the Leadership Network Innovation Series presents case studies and insights from leading practitioners and pioneering churches that are successfully navigating the ever-changing streams of spiritual renewal in modern society. Each book offers *real* stories, about *real* leaders, in *real* churches, doing *real* ministry. Readers gain honest and thorough analyses, transferable principles, and clear guidance on how to put proven ideas to work in their individual settings.

With the assistance of Leadership Network—and the Leadership Network Innovation Series—today's Christian leaders are energized, equipped, inspired, and enabled to multiply their own dynamic kingdom-building initiatives. And the pace of innovative ministry is growing as never before.

For additional information on the mission or activities of Leadership Network, please contact:

LEADERSHIP NETWORK®

800-765-5323 • w eadnet.org